ALPHA MALE

Who They Are, How They Think, What They Want

How to Attract, Meet, Marry & Train One

By XX and XY

Perennial Press
314 East Central Ave.
Moorestown, NJ 08057

Printed in the United States of America

Library of Congress Cataloging-in-Publication Data
XX and XY

ISBN: 978-0-6151-7509-6

1. Men
2. Dating
3. Alpha Males
4. Marriage

For **A. F. A. D**.

CONTENTS

Introduction

1. Identifying the Alpha Male

2. Finding an Alpha Male

3. Dating an Alpha Male

4. How to Make an Alpha Male
   Fall in Love with You

5. Getting an Alpha Male to Propose Marriage

6. Training Your Alpha Male

7. 101 Training Tips for Your Alpha Male

8. Happiness with an Alpha Male

9. The Alpha Male at Work:
   Where Alpha Males Rule

10. Key Points to Remember

    Epilogue

INTRODUCTION

Alpha Males are born, not made.

Winning is built into the Alpha Male — he succeeds in virtually every area far more often than other males. Alpha Males are leaders, good providers, and highly protective of their pack (or, in the case of human ones, family). An Alpha Male stands at the very top of the food chain. Life with an Alpha Male is living large, exciting, interesting, rewarding, fun, and entertaining.

Alpha Males are also far more dominant and strongly directed than other males. In several important ways they are entirely different from all other males. If you are interested in an Alpha Male – married to one, going out with, or interested in finding and sharing your life with one – you will need special knowledge. That is what this book is about.

An understanding of dog and wolf packs will help you quickly to grasp the essence of the human Alpha Male, because there are many strong parallels.

This book tells you how to find that top-of-the-pack Alpha Male, cause him to fall in love with you, propose marriage, and with proper handling, become a wonderful husband. Nothing is as much fun as being married to a properly civilized Alpha Male. But it doesn't happen automatically. You have to train him.

This book will tell you all you need to know. It is packed with practical information from both male and female points of view.

The first part of the book deals with identifying your Alpha Male (is he the real thing?), then setting up the situation so he will decide you are the one woman he wants and will propose marriage.

Men and dogs both operate in a hierarchy, with the most dominant male, called the Alpha Male, occupying the top position. This book explains how to identify, attract, marry, and train an Alpha Male (human) of your very own. This book tracks the close similarities between human and canine pack behavior in order to shed light on human Alpha Males.

But it doesn't stop there. Consider for a moment how dog and wolf packs are set up and run by an Alpha Male dog or wolf. Your Alpha Male (human) is identical in nearly every aspect. Both canine and human Alpha Males are hierarchical, territorial, brave, opportunistic, and fearless in defense of their pack.

Alpha Males are some of most desirable examples of the male. And more than half of this country is made up of women, many of whom would like nothing better than to find a truly terrific man, marry him, and have a wonderful life together. In spite of the alternatives – and today there are many, including living together outside the bonds of matrimony, remaining single, having serial monogamous relationships, forming enduring same-sex relationships, to name a few of the more obvious ones – many, perhaps even most, women still want a plain, fairly traditional marriage for a lifetime with one man. And they want this man to be the man of their dreams. For many, this means an Alpha Male.

What about women who are already married to Alpha Males and find their behavior confusing, frustrating, or even intimidating? They will find this book of interest too. It contains clearly presented concepts, which in many cases are the same as those used in dog training, which give step-by-step training tips for your Alpha Male. So who, exactly, is this Alpha Male? And why do so many women want one?

In a wolf pack, the pack members mostly don't hurt each other. They make threatening moves, and the other wolves back off.

The Alpha Male is the natural leader, the male who invariably rises to the top, or will — sometimes literally — die trying. He's the male who leads by example; the one that other males look up to (with trust, awe, or envy); the man most other men would most like for a buddy to hang out with. Although he will sometimes admit that he was wrong, an Alpha Male will never, never fully admit defeat. If momentarily defeated, he will always come back for one more try. He has supreme confidence in his ability to make things ultimately turn out as he wants them to even when things go wrong. He is the one who, in a meeting, will pass on his emotional state to the others simply because he is powerful and others pay attention to him. And he is the male who considers it his right to have the most desirable woman as his mate, the best job with himself in charge of it, the best house, the best possessions, and the top ancillary accomplishments.

In short, the Alpha Male possesses some of the most desirable qualities any male could possibly have: intelligence; courage; optimism; confidence; and the ability to lead, to make decisions, and to command absolute loyalty from his followers. Alpha Males have, in addition, that difficult-to-define quality, a particular type of attractiveness, even magnetism, to both men and women, usually summed up in the word *cool.*

Ipse Dixit
ALPHA MALES IN THEIR OWN WORDS

"I'm an aware Alpha Male – meaning I have some characteristics some might say are feminine qualities. I observe things more than most men, I pay attention to detail, in my work at least. That's what makes me a good medical doctor. What's different about me is that I'm aware of what's underneath and the undercurrent, and I'm aware how thin the veneer is."

A true story of an Alpha Male still under the age of thirty:

"When I grew up I was always playing video games. It's a great outlet for an aggressive nature. Not to promote aggression, but you play a video game and you get to shoot people and kill them and fly planes. You can jump further and run faster. With these video games you can effectively do all these things that you could not normally do, and you can compete doing them.

"For me winning was always the clue to it. Once I beat a computer game I never picked it up again. And it was important for me that I did win. For me, winning was everything. With the earlier computer games you couldn't really play against other players that much, so you were just competing against the computer. Eventually you'd beat it or get to a stage where you couldn't, in which case you'd try it again.

Some Alpha Males bloom late. Usually quiet and sometimes introverted – considered "nerds" — they possess extraordinary powers of concentration and observation, and have deep interests. They may spend all their spare time playing computer games rather than football. Sometimes they do both.

When they break fully into their chosen lives, they succeed brilliantly on their own terms.

"I always wanted to be a commodities trader, ever since I first thought about it. After college I went to New York and got an interview for a job on the trading floor. It was a stress interview. There was a lot of math and interesting problems. The trading floor is perhaps the largest concentration of Alpha Males you will ever see anywhere. It is entirely men that are driven and competitive. And they're all competing for the same money, same positions. So I was asked in the interview on-the-spot questions to try to simulate a little bit the stress on the floor. They actually didn't care what my answers were, although I didn't know it at the time. All they cared about was how I'd handle the stress.

"I did fine; I didn't lose my cool. For example they'd say, 'What's thirteen times seventeen?'— you're not given a pencil and paper and this is in the middle of all these other interview questions and you're expected to answer it on the spot — 'Come on! Come on! Come on! What's thirteen times seventeen? What is it?' That kind of thing. You finally come up with an answer and they say, 'Are you sure? What's your confidence in that? Let's put some money on that as to whether or not that's right.' And someone is actually asking you to put money on the table to bet on whether you have confidence in your answer.

"Then the next question is thrown at you: 'How many square miles are in Mexico?' I had no idea; I gave them a guess, twelve thousand square miles. Then the next question: 'Okay, that's an estimate; do you think it's more or less than that number?' I told them I didn't know. 'Okay, I want you to come up with an amount of money you'd be willing to put on that, for every thousand miles that you are off.' It was a stress interview, getting into risk. So I answered all of these questions and I got through the process.

"Then they called me back for another interview and another; these were not as difficult as the first time. Then they said I would be told whether or not I was going to be hired the next time I came back. At the end of it they said, 'We like you, we think you're smart enough for this, but some of the guys are concerned that you might be a bit of a pussy.' I was taken aback. I was pissed, shocked, surprised. 'It's between you and some other guy,' they said, 'so we'll have to think about it and get back to you.'

"This was a job I really wanted, and pretty much needed, too. It was a dream job for me. I would get to clerk on the floor and become a commodities trader; what I always wanted to do was be a commodities trader. Talked to my parents; decided I had to do something aggressive to make it clear I could be physically aggressive as well as sharp enough for the job.

"We came up with a plan. I had an old picture of myself wrestling, one of the rare pictures in which I was winning, and I'm pinning some guy to the floor in this picture. It's a black and white photo; I look really tough and strong. Took this picture, which was about wallet size, and blew it up to about a foot-and-a-half by two feet. I came in uninvited the following day, the exact same time as my previous interview; walked in, waited for the traders to get in. They came in; I slapped the picture on the table and said, 'Look, this is me wrestling in high school. Is this aggressive enough for you? Either you give me the job now, or I'm going to walk out the door; don't bother to call me.' They said, 'All right, you're hired.'

"They then proceeded to take the picture and put it up on their dartboard. There was no question that they were still in control. So that was how I got my first job. "

When he had worked there two years, the young man quit his job. He convinced his parents to mortgage their house and lend him several hundred thousand dollars, with which he bought a seat on the New York Stock Exchange and began to do his own trading. He repaid the loan in full within three months, and set himself a goal, since reached, to become a millionaire before he turned twenty-five. His next goals are to become a billionaire by age forty – and to find the woman of his dreams and marry her. Most would agree he fits the category of "cool."

Ipse Dixit
ALPHA MALES IN THEIR OWN WORDS

"Men are remarkably primitive and selfish. Food and sex are primary, but men also love going to the toilet. They just sit there and read and have a grand time where they're just away from everybody else, away from all demands and requests. On the toilet, he's given permission to be not bothered because he's in the bathroom."

What makes Alpha Males so cool? Many people begin to really study them in high school. They're the ones everyone watches. Guys envy and admire them; girls would like to date them. What sets the Alpha Males apart from the rest of the pack? For one thing, Alpha Males always seem to be on the move, going someplace, doing something – and they always have a group of followers who go along, and copy their style of speech, dress, and behavior. Alpha Males have high energy – even if that energy is bottled up and contained, you have the feeling it could bust out at any moment. Alpha Males already possess one of the most important of social skills, that of pack leadership and pack management.

The Alpha Male high school guy almost never goes after girls; he just stands still, lets the girls surround him, then chooses the Alpha Female (prettiest, most socially adept, sexiest). Because of his own universally acknowledged attractiveness, he doesn't have to risk failure by pursuing and, therefore, never gets turned down, adding to his aura of invincibility. Women who know this can use it to their advantage in capturing the attention of and training an Alpha Male.

As an Alpha Male's reputation for being cool grows, his skills
develop and deepen. Others follow; so he leads. He is often good
at sports, so he unites the team by his personality; he may edit
the school newspaper and influence everyone on it with his
style. An Alpha Male often doesn't even seem aware of his
power over others. He remains closely focused on the project at
hand – winning the game, whatever it may be – and the others
follow his lead.

The Alpha Male is loyal and demands absolute loyalty from his
"pack" – his wife, children, teammates, and everyone else he
leads, provides for, and protects. He is loyal to his buddies or his
girlfriend, so he protects them (by standing up for them or
sometimes even by punching someone out if needed). An Alpha
Male will not willingly let down his pack, honor being a vital

component to his character. This point bears remembering, because the Alpha Male's natural need for respect, and his sense of honor, will give his handler a tool for commanding respect from this naturally dominant creature. Honor – that is, respect – is very important to the Alpha Male. He behaves honorably in virtually every case, which is to say that he leads, provides for, and protects his pack.

Ipse Dixit
ALPHA MALES IN THEIR OWN WORDS

"I'm a single man — late twenties — I don't want to sleep with hundreds of women; I want to meet a special idealized woman. I have all kinds of ideas in my mind about what I want. It's not that I'm afraid of growing old and dying alone; I have plenty of friends. But I have a tremendous desire to find that right person out there and to get married to her. And this is despite those undercurrents of wanting to sleep with all of the women I have ever come across in my entire life."

Alpha Males are almost invariably exciting to be around, interesting, not petty or mean-spirited, original in their thinking, and generally fun to be with. Alpha Males do their job (lead, provide, and protect) and they expect their women to do theirs (create an ordered and comforting haven to which they can withdraw in between bouts of dominance against the world at large).

There are some things Alpha Males are *not* good at, however. Do not expect him to stop the car and ask directions when lost. That would show weakness; although not a conscious thought, an Alpha Male knows at some deep level that he must *never* let another male know he is vulnerable or the other male will attack him and carry off his women and children and eat them. Do not expect him to pick up his dirty clothes when he steps out of them and leaves them on the floor – he is marking his territory. Even if you train him to be neater, he will still leave something here or there to show exactly which Alpha Male lives here. (The comic writer Dave Barry once pointed out that men today believe they have evolved fully because they no longer just step out of their dirty clothes wherever they may be standing; today they know that they are supposed to put them in a neat pile for the Laundry Fairy to pick up.)

Ipse dixit
ALPHA MALES IN THEIR OWN WORDS

"At Oxford University, one of the students had looked up some law from medieval times that said that all students were required to be served two beers before sitting their exam. He demanded that his professor comply with this ancient rule. The professor looked this up in the by-laws of the college and saw that this was indeed true. The professor showed up before the exam with the two beers. And then he fined the student for not wearing his sword.

"Apparently in civilized society, men would walk around with their sword. If you were a gentleman, you were expected to wear your sword and be able to defend your honor. That constant underlying threat brings civility, and men treat each other in a civil way. We live by these rules with other men, and women really do not enter into it. What a woman wants has nothing to do with this relationship."

Do not expect him to be your confidant or hold cozy chats with you about your relationship, your inner feelings, or your worries (even if he happens to share them). It's not that he cannot do these things; rather, he doesn't want to, and forcing him to will create tensions that can be avoided by handling the situation in another way. Handled correctly, you'll be able to get the help you need without creating tensions. (More about this later.)

One further important point: As will be made clear further on, the female who chooses an Alpha Male *must never relinquish her position of equality*, or she can be crushed (emotionally, if in no other way). The woman who chooses to take on an Alpha Male as a life partner will need to learn procedures for maintaining her position of equality with him. It is a natural tendency of all Alpha Males to dominate; if unchecked, this domination can become an escalated version of itself – he becomes not just dominating but *domineering* – that is, oblivious to the wishes, needs, and requirements of anyone else. When this is allowed to happen, an Alpha Male loses respect for the person he is able to beat down verbally or through body language. Both dogs and men behave in nearly identical ways in this respect. Later chapters will deal with the tools and procedures for maintaining your position of equality with an Alpha Male.

> *An Alpha Male wants his woman to have interests of her own, of course. But she must always, always be interested in him. He will be quite pleased (even a tiny bit smug?) if she shows him preference over their children – remember that Neil Diamond song with the lines: "She leaves the children – Ain't it right, ain't it right, ain't it right?"*

This book tells where you are most likely to find an Alpha Male; the best strategy for attracting, meeting, and dating one; tactics for causing the Alpha Male of your choice to fall in love with and propose to you; how to avoid being taken for granted or belittled by a partly-trained (and dominant) Alpha Male; dos and don'ts for keeping your Alpha Male happy; and much more. You will even learn how to win an argument with an Alpha Male (yes, it *is* possible, at least some of the time).

> *Studies have shown that men who serve in elite regiments of the Armed Forces — Rangers, Navy Seals, or Green Berets, for example – have far fewer instances of sickness than other men, even when exposed to severe conditions of cold and deprivation.*

You don't have to be the most beautiful or perfect woman to captivate and win an Alpha Male. But you do have to know how to go about it. You can have a spectacularly good marriage with an Alpha Male – more exciting, more fun, more engaging, and nearly always more financially rewarding than with any lesser male. But Alpha Males of the human variety need training and good management, just as their canine counterparts do. Because they are so much more energetic and usually physically gifted than ordinary males, if left untrained or badly handled, things can go wrong. This book will tell you step by step how to manage the whole process of meeting, entrancing, and marrying an Alpha Male of your choice — and what to do to correct problems if they arise.

Ipse Dixit
ALPHA MALES IN THEIR OWN WORDS

"If women weren't around, men would be peeing on trees. When you're a man the world's a urinal. A banker and lawyer who commute to New York City daily for their jobs were watching a dog marking his territory by peeing on a tree. One said, musingly, 'You know, that's not such a bad idea.'"

Keeping an eye on the funny side of things plays a big part in creating and maintaining a happy life with an Alpha Male. As an old Quaker woman who had had a long and extremely happy marriage to an Alpha Male said to a young woman, "You're getting married my dear? You'll *love* it! *They're so <u>funny</u>!*" The better you understand men, the better you can deal productively with what can otherwise be merely frustrating behavior; it becomes comprehensible and, increasingly, actually amusing and interesting instead. You no longer need to battle against the male's instinctive behavior, instead you can use it to get what *you* want. And, in the process, you can create a good or even great marriage with a happy, productive husband to share life with.

This book talks about real, factual, observed behavior. But as the ancient Romans (one of the great sources of Alpha Males, from Julius Caesar to the gladiators) said, "*Ridentem dicere verum, quid vetat.*" (What harm in telling the truth while laughing?)

This book tells in ten chapters:

- What are the chief characteristics of an Alpha Male? Is he a true Alpha Male? – The Common Alpha Male Characteristics and Assessment Test: a 12-point Questionnaire. Is an Alpha Male right for you?

- Alpha Male imposters and also-rans: How to recognize the real thing and avoid the imposters.

- Where can you find an Alpha Male? Some of the most likely ways to meet one, and some surprising places to try.

- How to date an Alpha Male. Pitfalls to avoid. The best way to win his attention.

- Should you have sex before marriage? Advice straight from Alpha Males themselves, and some information and conclusions that may astound you.

- How to cause an Alpha Male to fall in love with you.

- How to get an Alpha Male to propose.

- What to do if the Alpha Male of your choice hasn't proposed within six months or so. A practical strategy for making it happen.

- Making it work with your Alpha Male – what to do if it isn't working.

- 101 Training Tips for your Alpha Male. Dos and Don'ts that make life easier for the trainer and more fun for both of you.

- How to make your Alpha Male back off if he tries to intimidate or demean you.

- How to keep your Alpha Male happy in the long term after the initial euphoria has worn off (very important).

- The Alpha Male in the work-place; how to handle Alpha Male bosses and co-workers. How to marry an Alpha Male boss.

About the authors.

The information in this book is the combined observations of two people. XX is a woman who remained unmarried for longer than most women do.

Sometimes asked why she had never married, she had a ready stock reply: *"Oh, it was a series of narrow escapes."* This worked fine until she said it to one of the supreme Alpha Males of his generation, twice Olympic gold medal winner in Three-day Eventing, the most grueling of equine sports; he assumed an overly innocent expression and asked, *"On whose part?"*

For most of those unmarried years XX dated a wide spectrum of males – the sample runs to the many hundreds with proposals of marriage at the rate, on average, of one per year. (Incidentally, almost any woman of average looks and intelligence who uses the rules of this book will likely have many proposals of marriage if she doesn't marry immediately.)

A dog trainer with more than thirty years' experience, XX works with aggressive dogs and also trains registered service dogs for work with Alzheimer's patients in nursing homes. She is author of a dog-training book that has remained continually in print since the mid-1990s. The book features photographs of many pit bulls used with great success as pet therapy dogs in hospitals and nursing homes.

XX is also author of three books on training horses and riders, one of which also has remained in continual print since 1995 and was endorsed by the (Olympic) United States Equestrian Team.

XX spent several years in marketing and public relations work in New York City as account executive for a leading public relations firm and as editorial assistant and director of public relations for a well-known publishing house. She has also worked in television production and film production, and has coached authors and others for television appearances on programs that include the *Today Show*. She has been published in the *New York Times* and many newspapers and magazines. She was a member of the editorial board of *New China Magazine* in New York. XX worked in Washington DC as a legislative aide to U.S. Senator Samuel J. Ervin, Jr. (d, NC) in the hearings leading to Watergate.

She is listed in Marquis *Who's Who In America*.

Her co-author, XY, himself the quintessential Alpha Male, had a thirty-year career as an Army officer (he enlisted two years early by misstating his age, moved up in rank through battlefield merit to the rank of Lt. Colonel, and won among other awards the Silver Star for heroism on Omaha Beach in World War II). His own life, and that of his men, depended on his absolute understanding of the young men under his command and knowing how to motivate them in specific ways under extreme conditions. His subsequent career as Chief of Detectives for a large East Coast city gave him leadership over 180 detectives in a high-crime metropolis.

A photograph of one of the former young lieutenants who served under him in the U.S. Army Infantry (now the four-star General in charge of all U.S. Army European operations), shaking his hand at the Commemoration of D-Day fifty years later registers the respect on the younger man's face that borders on awe — a younger Alpha Male recognizing and paying tribute to an older Alpha Male.

The authors of this book married each other and began comparing notes. This book contains everything they know about Alpha Males, from both male and female perspectives.

1.

IDENTIFYING THE ALPHA MALE

In this chapter you will learn how to identify a genuine Alpha Male, discover his most prominent characteristics, and find out what motivates him. You will learn what equipment to use — and what not to use — as you begin to train him. You will explore some similarities that all Alpha Males (human) share with wolves and dogs. And you'll consider the *non*-Alpha Males, many of whom try hard to appear to be Alphas but are not. You'll be able to decide if an Alpha Male is right for you — *they are not for everyone.*

How can you be certain that a man you are interested in – one you'll meet if you follow the guidelines in this book, or a man you know already – is a genuine Alpha Male? How can you differentiate between the real Alpha Male and the males who seem on the surface to be, but in fact are not?

Here is a questionnaire to help you determine if the male you are considering is a genuine Alpha Male. If you answer *yes* to all twelve points, he's the genuine article. Otherwise, he's not a true Alpha Male, although he may have some Alpha Male tendencies.

Questionnaire: *Is He a Genuine Alpha Male?*

1. He never fully admits defeat while there is the remotest chance of success, even if it takes him many tries to accomplish his goal. Even when temporarily defeated, he will always come back for one more try when circumstances change in his favor.

2. He keeps his focus on the task at hand. He is nearly impossible to distract from his purpose once he has set his course of action.

3. Other males follow and are influenced by him. They copy his attitude, speech pattern, dress, or other aspect of his general style. They try to look, sound, and act like him.

4. He is completely oblivious to point three, above. He just goes about the job at hand. He never copies the style of his followers. He doesn't self-consciously lead; he simply does what he wants, and others follow.

5. He looks out for his male buddies. He will stand up for them in an argument or fight (he will punch someone out physically or verbally if necessary).

6. He takes his time to determine the best course of action if there is time. He assesses a situation with a cool head, determines the best way of achieving his goals, and moves ahead when he is ready in a way that is almost unstoppable.

7. He can replicate point six, above, with lightning speed if necessary. Once he is in action, he does not second-guess himself.

8.   He never dwells on mistakes. When a result is unsatisfactory but he himself decides the goal cannot be achieved, he takes note of it, determines the lessons to be learned from it, then dismisses it from his mind.

9.   He is attractive to both men (who want to copy him or hang out with him as a buddy) and to women.

10.   He is protective of his women and children. He would literally die to protect them.

11.   He is not upset by change (anywhere *except* in his own safe den, where he goes to recharge himself).

12.   He looks on change as opportunity, and immediately begins thinking how to turn it to the advantage of himself and his pack.

Among wolves, the process of taking over the leadership position of an existing pack whose leader has been killed requires that the new Alpha Male wolf demonstrate his courage and fearlessness. He must stand without flinching as, one after another, the males of the pack run at him, fangs bared, in apparent attack, only to veer off or stop short at the last instant. The process can go on for many hours. Only after he has proved himself is there a chance that the Alpha Female, widow of the original leader, will indicate that she likes what she sees. She may nuzzle the new leader, put her paw over his back, or allow him to show affection in the same way.

Characteristics of an Alpha Male:

There are a number of similarities common to all Alpha Males, as well as some differences. The single most apparent characteristic of all Alpha Males, whether human or canine, is this: *The Alpha Male must lead.* It isn't an optional choice for him; it is a necessity. If he finds himself in a position other than leader of the pack, he will try and try and try again, until he topples the leader of the pack and becomes leader himself. His only options are to lead, to die trying to ascend to the number-one position, or to go off and start his own pack elsewhere. Take note, however, that Alpha Males do not remain lone wolves for long if they can help it. They will create a pack by attracting an Alpha Female, or take over a pack in which the leader has been killed.

The human Alpha Male looks at uncertainty as a continuing state of existence, a constant reality of life. When he makes a mistake, he takes note of the mechanics of the event, but he's immediately over it. This ability to recover quickly sets the Alpha Male apart from all others. Where an Alpha Male looks at uncertainty as a chessboard of opportunity, the follower looks at uncertainty and becomes puzzled, and may fixate on the mistake, mulling it over and over. The Alpha Male's motto, by contrast, might be: *"Don't gloat and don't regret. Just do what needs to be done. And move on."*

The human Alpha Male will never truly accept that another male has the right to boss him around. He will never blindly accept the judgment of another male over his own. No other male's opinion is considered more trustworthy than his own.

Among human Alpha Males, even in military service where orders are a way of life, he will find a way to withhold some part of his apparent obedience from a superior officer if he does not respect his judgment, by a word, his tone of voice, the timing of his response, or a detail of how he wears his uniform. An Alpha Male will nearly always be a superb leader of men; he shows by example, the surest way to win his men's respect. In interactions with his own men (Alpha Males nearly always rise to positions of command) he will be a leader in whom his men place absolute confidence.

An Alpha Male is exceedingly good at certain things, and at the same time must not, under pain of disaster, be expected to be or become something alien to his nature. This book will deal with this subject in detail.

What do men want?

Poor Sigmund Freud never did figure out the answer to the question that kept him awake nights for his entire life: *What do women want?*

Luckily men are much simpler creatures to figure out (despite the fact that some have admirable intellects). *We know exactly what men want.*

Men and dogs are nearly identical in much of their behavior. Both are primarily interested in two things: food and sex. Both move straight ahead in a direct line, rarely looking from side to side in pursuit of these two commodities. They of course have other interests, but they are driven forward by these two primal forces.

> *In fights, the hair on the back of an Alpha Male dog's neck rises, which makes him appear taller. When he is trying to intimidate another male without fighting, his fur goes up, his tail is held straight up, and he walks stiffly and slowly, standing as tall as possible.*

If you understand these facts, you can go a long way toward persuading men to do what you want them to. This is important, because all men — especially the Alpha Male, who is quicker, usually physically stronger, and always more dominant than other men — need training. Otherwise they will move in a straight line toward food and sex without any modifying influence, which can be tiresome, alarming, or a downright pain in the neck.

> *Ipse Dixit*
> **ALPHA MALES IN THEIR OWN WORDS**
>
> *"Men are utterly clueless as to what is going on in the world. We observe nothing. Men live in a world that is far simpler that the one inhabited by women. We live in a world with none of the stealth, none of the cloak-and-dagger, none of the 'this person's trying to stab me in the back,' 'that person looked at me funny.'"*

What behavior cannot be separated from the Alpha Male?

Alpha Males of both human and canine species will fight off challengers to the death if need be, and they protect their mates and families without thinking there is any other option. They accept completely that everyone, both male and female in any group or structure (family or work, for instance) reports to them. They tend to amass large piles. Dogs amass territory by urinating on it; this then becomes their hunting territory, from which they feed their pack and themselves. Human Alpha Males amass money, sometimes trophy wives, possessions, honors, and accolades. Both move, for the most part, straight ahead, not looking to either side.

Ipse Dixit
ALPHA MALES IN THEIR OWN WORDS

"What makes a man choose the woman of his dreams for marriage?
The chemistry? I met her at a party. I thought she was beautiful. She had a wonderful personality. A giving, open smile. To me it was obvious that she was right up front. She was clearly a person without cunning or guile."

It follows that Alpha Males of both species are brave and courageous, acquisitive, protective, and loyal. They brook no interference with their decisions, which, as they see it, protect and guide their pack or family group.

If you happen to be a good dog trainer, you will already know much of the information in this book. Dog training, especially as it relates to the top dog of the pack, is quite similar to the training of the Alpha Male of the human variety.

The importance of greeting to an Alpha Male.

In a wolf pack, when the Alpha Male leads his followers out to hunt for food, it is a reality that sometimes one or more members of the pack are killed and never return. There is, therefore, a celebration, called a *full wolf greeting*, each time the leader and his pack return, in which the lower members approach the Alpha Male and by body language (wagging tails, facial grins, lowering of ears and head) one by one greet the leader. If a member of the pack is missing, the other members reaffirm their place in the hierarchy relative to the Alpha Male by this behavior. Any pack members who stayed behind during the hunt — females who care for the cubs, for example – greet the Alpha Male and show joy at his return.

This behavior presents itself almost invariably in situations in which the Alpha Male has been absent for even a short time. A woman thinking of acquiring an Alpha Male, or who is already married to one, may want to take note of this hardwired behavior, because it is just as characteristic of the human Alpha Male as the canine.

> *This may seem a trivial point but it's not. This behavior is hardwired into your Alpha Male's inner feelings: Human Alpha Males like to be greeted as the conquering hero even when they have just been out on routine business. Greeting him with a smile and a friendly hug or squeeze of the hand every time he comes through the door is a good idea. Even if there are problems to be worked out, make the small effort to perform a welcoming greeting first.*

One mother married to an Alpha Male used to allow their three young children to go to meet their father's train at the station a block away when he returned from work. Every single time, before they were allowed to set off, she rehearsed a litany: they must not tell their father about their quarrels, they could not tell him about anything that made them upset or angry or vengeful, or ask him for presents. They were taught that meeting their father was a treat and they were taught to offer a friendly greeting to the Alpha Male of the family.

A word on training equipment:

The equipment used to train dogs differs from what you'll use in training the human Alpha Male. Note that a man's necktie is *not* analogous to a dog's collar and leash. Rather, the necktie is a stand-in for a piece of his anatomy that means a lot to him.

To test this theory, do two things: First, try to pull an Alpha Male by his tie. He will not follow you. Second, give an Alpha Male a tie that is too short. He will not wear it, because he will be embarrassed.

Another test: Keep your eye on a man's hand when he is trying to diminish another male verbally. He will quite often slowly stroke his tie as he speaks, and when he has driven his argument into the heart of his adversary, will give the end of the tie a little flip upward and outward before walking away.

Ipse Dixit
ALPHA MALES IN THEIR OWN WORDS

"Men see women and they want to sleep with them. It's the conquest including the sexual act. Not the conquest alone. A friend of mine slept with a supermodel. Afterward he proceeded to call every friend he knew and tell them he'd slept with her. It had nothing to do with possibly damaging her reputation. He was extremely proud of the fact that he had done it."

The role of the Alpha Male in a dog pack.

Here is how it works in a dog pack: The top male of the dog pack, the Alpha dog, is responsible for the safety of his entire pack, consisting of his mate, offspring, and any stray bodies he happens to be fond of, usually but not always additional females and very junior males. The Alpha dog can bite or threaten any other member of the pack, and sometimes does so just to keep everyone in line and obedient to his authority.

To control pack members, an Alpha Male uses body language and threats in addition to actual biting. To make a direct challenge to another male, the Alpha Male stands squarely facing his adversary and makes eye contact at the other dog's level. Sometimes this is enough to avert an actual fight; the lesser dog lowers his eyes, lowers his head, and walks stiffly away (one novelist described it as "like a table, walking"). The victorious Alpha Male then scratches the dirt with his hind and sometimes also his front feet, leaving his adrenalin-laden scent (a dog's pads sweat) as a readable sign to all that he was here and he triumphed.

"Standing over" is one of the tools the Alpha Male dog uses; he stands with his head and neck directly over that of a dog he wants to intimidate, and freezes in this position until the junior dog lowers his ears (this shows that he is no longer taking cues from the world at large, but now from the Alpha Male), lowers his head (he becomes both symbolically and physically lower than the Alpha), and slinks away, tail between his legs (putting his tail out of harm's way in case the Alpha decides to chomp on it as a parting comment).

Male brains, even before birth, develop differently from female brains. From birth males are less able to "read" facial expressions or tone of voice.

In general, males are much better at feats of strength, agility, or endurance, so they are good at fighting, wars, competitions in general, and football. And males are less affected by the gruesome effects of mayhem.

A huge taxi driver in Washington, DC, asked what his prior work had been, said he had been a linebacker for the Green Bay Packers and been injured badly enough so he could never play again. He said, "I loved the game! I loved it more than anything in the world." Asked what aspect of the game he missed most, he thought quite a while and said, "I loved that moment when you heard them bones breaking. I loved that sound."

An Alpha Male dog may, as the ultimate insult, actually urinate on another male dog's head (human Alpha Males also do this, substituting bellowed insults or a punch in the nose.) A truly humble dog near or at the bottom of the pack structure – a puppy, for instance – will actually roll over, exposing his belly to the Alpha Male, thus showing his abject self-abasement – ("do-what-you-will-with-me"), and pee all over himself. The Alpha Male accepts, and demands, this obedience. But he does not respect those he can intimidate. Please note an interesting point: He cannot intimidate the true Alpha Female because she will not allow it, although she does not directly confront him. (More about this later.)

Ipse Dixit
ALPHA MALES IN THEIR OWN WORDS

"My closest male friend from college some twenty-five years ago and his wife joined my wife and me for a day at the beach. The women went off together looking for beach flowers, and my friend and I were left alone on beach chairs. We had a wonderful, a memorably fine, afternoon together. I read the paper and he slept. It was memorable because we were just left alone. It was peaceful and quiet.

"It's possible that a man likes to be with another man even if they don't talk or interact at all for the same reason dogs or wolves do – that is, if you are alone, you are vulnerable to attack. But with another male in some sort of proximity, there is a peacefulness that comes from being less vulnerable to attack."

The Alpha Male wolf's job as pack leader is four-fold. He breeds with the Alpha female; protects her while she is carrying, nursing, and raising their cubs; protects her and the rest of the pack by making the decisions that keep them safe from destruction; and leads hunting expeditions that keep them all fed. The role of the Alpha Male of the human type is remarkably similar.

Alpha Males—the human ones –are likely to order steak rare. Hardly any of them, as pointed out years ago, will voluntarily hunt down a quiche and eat it.

Dogs fed raw meat are typically more aggressive than those fed dry kibble made from wheat and byproducts.

How to Identify an Alpha Dog.

You can spot the Alpha dog when just a nursing puppy. He will be first to the milk supply, pushing his siblings out of the way. You can observe him as an eight-week old puppy, barely able to walk. If you turn even such a young Alpha puppy on his back, he will struggle valiantly to turn right-side up, even though you are fifty times bigger than he is. And, what is a sure sign: He will not give up trying. At first his concern is for himself. As he grows, he expands his interest to include siblings, pushing them around in play so they will accept that he occupies a place above them in pack order. Alpha Male humans are motivated in the same way.

> *The next L.L.Bean or Orvis catalog you receive showing puppies sprawled over a dog bed, take note which puppy is staring straight into the camera with his ears up. This is the Alpha puppy. He is on the job, watching out for the safety of his 'pack.'*

Humor and the Alpha Wolf.

When the wolf pack goes out to hunt, studies have shown that only about once in five times do they succeed in bringing back food for the waiting pack. This means everyone is tired, perhaps cold and wet, and in addition, hungry, including not only the hunters but the females and cubs left at home.

On return, if one of the hunters snarls angrily as if to say, "Some leader *you* are," the Alpha Male may kill him, effectively removing him from the gene pool. So this characteristic is unlikely to be passed on to a new generation.

But if a Beta Male cavorts about acting silly, to lighten everyone's mood and amuse the cubs and take their minds off their hunger, the Alpha Male approves. (An Alpha will not himself usually do this, however.) Humor demonstrably does exist among dogs and wolves, and non-Alpha Males who have it are favored by posterity.

> *Do human Alpha Males have a sense of humor? Yes, most do. But they are not the ones who act silly to entertain the troops. Humor for the Alpha Male generally is evoked when a rival or adversary gets his just comeuppance.*

Are there drawbacks?

Human Alpha Males can, if left untrained, become domineering, even bullying, oblivious to the wishes of anyone else, deaf to principled disagreement, single-minded in pursuit of a goal to

> *Human Alpha Males strew their used laundry about the house for a very good reason. They are marking their territory.*

the extent that much else is lost (time for children, interest in needs of individual family members for instance). The Alpha Male is perhaps the most single-minded animal on earth. Alpha Males can be infuriating because when they are leading in one direction they are hard to stop (or even to slow down in many cases), and it may be next to impossible to make one change course once his plan is in action.

Fortunately, Alpha Males can be trained. A trained and civilized Alpha Male makes an outstanding husband. Handled properly and kindly, Alpha Males are among the most trustworthy and endearing of partners. Just be sure to keep in mind that it will be a partnership of two *very different* creatures – one might consider an Alpha Male husband and his female counterpart almost of different species.

Due to the Alpha Male's greater drive, intelligence, and need for respect, if his trainer makes errors in handling him, the results will be far worse than they would be with another male – indeed in some cases they can be disastrous.

An Alpha Male's behavior is built on a kind of quicksand. This book will look closely at the insecurity that underlies the Alpha Male's behavior. We will consider the Alpha Male at three periods of his life: In his earliest years, when Alpha behavior is readily apparent and unguarded; in the prime years, at the height of his powers, when a woman might consider acquiring one for marriage; and in the last years, when physical strength decreases but Alpha nature and behavior does not.

Runners-up and imposters: How can you tell the true Alpha Male from other high achievers?

There are many males who appear to be happy enough in subservient positions — look in any corporation, for instance – men who quite contentedly take orders from another male (and in some instances, a female). Even if they growl and moan about it on lunch hour or to their wives, these non-Alpha Males won't risk doing anything about it.

In what ways does an Alpha Male differ from other high-achieving males? *Unless his fundamental and defining drive is to lead, protect, and provide, he isn't a true Alpha Male, no matter how great his achievements.* Here are some of the runners-up and imposters:

- *Trailblazers*

Some examples of high-achieving non-Alpha Males include Albert Einstein (world-shaking scientist but responsible for a terrible home life that included divorce from his first wife, mother of his sons, and marriage to a second wife during which he fathered an illegitimate daughter adopted out; and many of the best-known and bravest explorers and adventurers, including Sir Edmund Hillary (gone from home for months or years at a time, and first to climb Mount Everest to the top), Admiral Byrd (discoverer of the South Pole), and Paul Gaugin (one of the world's great painters, who ditched his wife and family to go paint in Polynesia).

These men and others like them could be termed Trailblazers. The achievements of Trailblazers are often very great, but they are not Alpha Males. They do what they want, but they do so without concern for the good of the pack, and often at the great expense of their family or wives.

- *Beta Males*

Think sidekick: Butch Cassidy to the Sundance Kid, Tonto to the Lone Ranger (although some say Tonto was actually the brains of the operation but wisely allowed the Lone Ranger to *think* he was in charge), Robin to Batman. Most Alpha Males have quite a number of sidekicks who hang out with them and, insofar as they are able, copy their style of speech, action, dress, attitude. There is nothing wrong with marrying a Beta Male — some awfully nice men are Betas — but if you are looking for an Alpha, you will be disappointed.

- *Charismatic Phonies*

Another species of non-Alpha Male is the Charismatic Phony. He seems, at first look, to be a true Alpha Male – strongly directed, decisive, fun to be with, often chivalrous and good at making a woman feel cherished. But he is not the real thing.

In adversity, a true Alpha Male goes into action: He assesses the situation with a cool head, determines what he will do, and turns it to action. An Alpha Male positively thrives on challenge and difficulty. Changing conditions are his natural habitat – he likes change, because he is unequalled in finding the opportunity in every changing condition and making use of it to protect and provide for his pack. He does not, ever, give up until he has won the battle.

A Charismatic Phony, on the other hand, falls apart at the first sign of difficulty. He will want you to take over, bail him out, handle it for him. He will have abundant reasons that, at first, sound logical enough to convince the unwary that he needs your help "just this once" for unusual reasons that are not his fault. He can't rent a car or book plane tickets or deal with a leaking roof or discuss anything he doesn't find enjoyable (although by not discussing it he is putting the burden squarely on you).

The Charismatic Phony ducks responsibility for everything except what he likes doing, and leaves others to pick up the pieces for his foul-ups. A Charismatic Phony has perfected only one thing: His patter and attractiveness are designed to manipulate you into doing everything for him (in addition to what you already do).

- *Bullies*

Bullies can be hard to recognize, because at first they seem strong and directed, like Alpha Males. When you first meet them, Bullies make great efforts to gain your trust, and can work hard to make you like them. The key is 'at first,' because gradually bullies beat you up. They may not do it physically, but they can punch verbally, push you down with sneering comments, insult you in front of other people, and grind away at your self-esteem. And, of course, some bullies actually do beat up women physically.

As a rule, the reason a bully tries to drive you down has in fact nothing to do with *you*; it has to do only with himself. A bully knows, deep down (sometimes at a level so deep he may not consciously see it), that he is a jerk. He doesn't like himself. He projects this onto you. If he is unfaithful, he accuses you of cheating. If he is a coward, he accuses you of cowardice. Bullies systematically cut you off from other people you like or love – family, friends – by being angry or upset when you choose to be with them or even when you talk with them on the phone or Internet.

The more you try to please a bully, the more you try to build up his self-esteem, the more he hates you for it. His thinking, if it were conscious, goes something like this: "She likes (or loves) me, but I'm not worth much. She doesn't see that, therefore she's too stupid to see through me — she buys into my act that I put on to con people into thinking I'm cool and not a jerk. Anyone who would love somebody like me can't be worth much herself. Therefore she's second-rate herself, and is trying to con me into falling for her, so I'll smash her down for it." You can find yourself confused when the man who has been acting so wonderfully toward you gradually begins to demean you. If it happens once, call him on it. If it happens twice, walk out for good.

- *Wishful Thinkers*

Wishful Thinkers try their best to copy and replicate the behavior of true Alpha Males in an attempt to appear to be leaders; the giveaway is that no one actually follows them. Even though they repeat the phrases they hear Alpha Males use, dress like them, copy their gestures, or employ people to surround themselves with who function as their 'followers', they can readily be seen to be phonies.

An example is a former owner of one of the trendiest of catalog companies whose catalog makes him appear – in print at least – to be 'cool,' that is, an Alpha Male. But when the owner mismanaged and lost his company, he defrauded numerous customers while he hid behind Chapter 11. Then, without repaying the people who had previously sent him money for goods they never received, he opened his company anew, with all the same false promises implicit: "Buy these goods and you will be, by association, as cool as I am." An Alpha Male would not go back into business after restructuring without paying what he owed to his former loyal customers. Honor is important to the true Alpha Male. He would consider his customers part of his extended "pack."

Another example of a non-Alpha Male who tries to pass himself off as the genuine article failed in business several times, was bailed out by his father's money each time, then created a television show devoted to himself in which he humiliates the contestants daily and writes snide notes to his competitors.

In contrast, the genuine Alpha Male is someone like Paul Newman, who, when asked in his younger years why he didn't respond to the advances of the droves of beautiful women who pursued him, replied (a bit inelegantly), "Why go after hamburger when you've got steak at home?" If the "steak," his wife Joanne Woodward, objected to this description, she never let on, being one of the most successful Alpha Male trainers on record.

- *Blowhards*

Always 'just about to succeed' but never in fact actually achieving anything is the unmistakable sign of a blowhard. These men like to paint themselves as movers and shakers; they speak in grandiose terms of the successes they plan to make happen — and then *nothing* happens. The blowhard loves the trappings of power, but is essentially powerless. He is a taker, not a giver. He studies Alpha Males and tries to duplicate their style as he sees it, but he is really a loser in the realest sense of the word: He never wins.

- *Married Men*

Married men who try to date other women on the side are deceivers; they are fundamentally dishonest and unreliable. But they can make themselves seem extremely available. They often have money and want to spend it on the object of their attraction. It is easy to fall for their ploy, and it is the worst mistake you can make.

By definition, no married man who cheats on his wife, no matter what his reasons, is an Alpha Male. A married man is just that, married, with a promise to be faithful to his wife; and, by definition, to cheat, a married man has to deceive his wife.

He will deceive not only his wife but also the woman he is trying to entice into a relationship with him. Some of the most often used excuses are: "My wife cheats on me, so it doesn't matter," or "My wife and I have an understanding — we go our separate ways on sex," or "We're just staying together until the children are grown," or "My wife doesn't understand me," (or — the *best* one!) "I really love you, honey; and I plan to leave my wife and marry you, just as soon as the kids (are out of school / high school / college / have their law degrees / Ph.D.s)."

Some married men actually do divorce their first wives (the ones who put them through medical school by working years at a job they didn't like, while under the delusion that his degree would later provide for them both) and marry their mistresses. And a good many then go on and do it again and again.

> *It is a good idea to remember the following point: "The man who marries his mistress leaves a job opening."*

But what if a married man says, "Listen, I'm a good guy. My wife and I should never have married in the first place. I did the right thing and married her because [place excuse here]. Now I've found *you*, I don't want to lose you. You're the only woman

I've ever loved. I really want to marry you. I love you and I know you love me." What should you do in the face of this heartfelt plea?

If a married man really is in a bad marriage, let him end it honorably first before involving you. Tell him so in no uncertain terms, and without conditions (such as that you promise to marry him if he does). If he's unwilling to do this, you don't want him. Walk away and don't look back. It's a con job.

- *Self-centered Narcissist*

Often talented, these men are attractive because their intensely focused energy seems to hold some mystery and promise. Their pent-up energy seems at first to be that of an Alpha Male.

What are they so intense about? Themselves. And as long as you fit into what a Self-centered Narcissist wants to do himself, you may bask in the reflected glow. But you are in for a rude awakening if you ever want or need anything yourself. These are the men who allow you to work to put them through law school, then dump you for a younger model when you've served your purpose.

It can be found in smaller doses too. Here's an example. A woman accompanied a Self-centered Narcissist who is extremely knowledgeable about the Civil War to several of the battlefields. The trip took two days, and was interesting enough for her, but mainly of fascination to the male. On the drive back to New York, where each lived, the woman asked, as they were driving within a mile of her childhood home where her parents still lived, if they could stop for a half hour so she could see her parents. The Narcissist made up every excuse why they could not stop (he was expecting a phone call, he didn't like to drive when the late afternoon sun began to slant, she should just *go along with him this one time*, etc. etc.) Finally she gave up, because his whining had worked: The one thing she wanted had been pushed aside for the Self-centered Narcissist's convenience. His sulking, had she persevered, would have ruined the trip in any case.

Watch out if a Self-centered Narcissist accuses you of something you know is untrue. Narcissists project their own faults onto you. If he accuses you of being disloyal, for example, by being intimate with other men, he is probably himself double-timing you.

- *Type A Behaviorist*

High-energy, impulsive, often angry and sometimes abusive — this male is not to be confused with Alpha Males.

"Type A" behavior — prone to hot-headed outbursts and quick to anger — is *not* characteristic of the Alpha Male. (On the contrary, the Alpha Male is not likely to fly off the handle or have temper tantrums. He has great energy but doesn't dissipate it in easily aroused anger.)

The only thing the two have in common is a high level of energy. Where the Type-A male jumps in without thinking (he is just reacting at his most primitive level of aggression), an Alpha Male thinks before he acts (although sometimes with lightning speed) and uses intelligence, rational thought, and problem-solving in addition to aggression (where needed) to bring about a defined result. This process may change quickly as circumstances change, but an Alpha Male will never simply 'run to the corner and go off in all directions' as a Type-A Male does. (The Type-A's motto is *"Ready, Fire! Aim!"*)

- *Impotent Miniature Poodle*

No, this isn't *actually* a poodle, but he's the human equivalent of a little yapping dog, full of aggression. The only reason such men even get a mention is because they *are* aggressive, and some women might possibly confuse this aggression, even in this ridiculous form, with a trait belonging to Alpha Males, and think he could be an Alpha Male for that reason. He isn't. His aggression is the aggression of the impotent and powerless. He makes an annoying pest of himself by spitefulness and is given to petty rages against the unprotected. He's the one who hangs a loud clanging bell on his front porch to annoy the neighbors (as long as the neighbor is elderly, sick, or a widow), and when asked politely to stop, gives a nasty smirk and adds another bell, louder than the first.

He chooses a job he thinks will make him appear 'cool' — and does it moderately well; he becomes, for example, a second-rate architect. Essentially powerless, he is One of Nature's Bureaucrats: He seeks power by joining every committee that will let him join. His 'power' consists of *preventing other people from doing things*. He can be compared to the tiny dog who scratches the dirt backward for ten feet after he pees to show what a big dog he really is. These men are either simply laughable or pitiful, depending on your viewpoint; avoid them altogether.

Did you think that Mark Twain (Samuel Clemens) was happiest when he had written his humorous masterpiece Huckleberry Finn? *Wrong! An Alpha Male who doted on his wife and three daughters, Twain recalled his earlier days as a riverboat captain – a demanding job requiring an almost supernatural memory for every detail of hundreds of miles of the Mississippi River and riverbanks—as the happiest time of his entire life. The reason was simple: "When I gave an order it was followed instantly and without question," he said.*

<u>Famous Alpha Males</u>: Some of the genuine Alpha Males of the past are still admired today. Legendary jazz musician and composer Miles Davis, whose innovations to music rank at the very highest level, is still a beacon to young Alpha Males. So is

the American jazz drummer Abe Speller, who accompanied Europe's famous 'answer to Bob Dylan,' Kim Larsen, on a wildly successful three-year gig during which his family – his 'pack' – periodically joined him, then left to rejoin his family full-time and form a new group in the U.S. – his own choice on his own terms.

It is relatively easy to compile one's own list of famous Alpha Males throughout history: Simply look for the man others follow. A few who come readily to mind include great military generals like Alexander the Great, Robert E. Lee, and Douglas MacArthur, all of whom commanded intense loyalty from their troops; the football greats Joe Namath and Joe Montana; basketball legend Wilt Chamberlain of the Harlem Globetrotters; and the man whose name became synonymous with baseball, George Herman "Babe" Ruth; and Lou Gehrig. There is a reason these Alpha Males from another era have achieved iconic stature: Alpha Males, besides being high achievers, are usually vivid, memorable men.

Ipse Dixit
ALPHA MALES IN THEIR OWN WORDS

"The more I see of man, the more I love my dog."
—*Alexander the Great*

Warren Buffett stands almost alone among Alpha Males. He charted his own, highly original course through the treacherous seas of finance and succeeded brilliantly. After earning all those billions, he decided that he will *not* leave large fortunes to his children. One could speculate that he values development of the qualities of Alpha Males and Alpha Females over giving his children a life of unearned leisure. Could it be that he doesn't want his kids to become rich wimps?

Among actors who have earned a place in history, Clint Eastwood, Lee Marvin, and James Stewart (personally courageous as a fighter pilot in World War II) are worth noting. Categories including today's sports figures, musicians, trial attorneys, educators, inventors, founders of businesses or organizations, explorers, publishers, entrepreneurs, all present numerous famous examples. Brett Favre of the Green Bay Packers is a more recent example (when his father died shortly before an important game, his teammates heightened their performance and won a very difficult game for him).

All Alpha Males, whether canine or human, lead, provide, and protect their mate, children, and pack. Can a case be made for a male who simply did not meet the right woman and form a strong pack with her as his partner? Is it Albert Einstein's fault that he betrayed his wife? Did he simply marry the wrong woman in the first place?

A true Alpha Male never gives up on any course of action that matters to him. Forming a strong family unit is essential to all Alpha Males. Loyalty is essential to all Alpha Males. A strong sense of responsibility is inseparable from a true Alpha Male.

Notable examples of Alpha Males include Brian Urquhart (read *A Bridge Too Far* by Cornelius Ryan); George Patterson (*"Patterson of Tibet,"* who walked across China in the 1940s, fought with the ferocious Tibetan *Khamba* tribes against the invading Chinese, and filmed it as the award winning documentary *Raid Into Tibet)*; and entrepreneur and inventor Joe

Winston, a brilliant strategist responsible for advances in bringing NET (NeuroElectric Therapy), a new method of curing, not merely treating, addictions, into the mainstream. And of course there's George Gip, the star football player in that iconic 1940s movie, *Knute Rockne, All American,* who, as he lay dying, asked his coach to "win just one for the Gipper." Make your own list.

> *Thomas Edison, when asked if he had become discouraged during the first two thousand unsuccessful attempts prior to inventing the lightbulb, replied: "What are you talking about? I invented the lightbulb. It just happened to be a two-thousand-step process." Confidence and optimism, dogged determination, a will to succeed, and a positive mindset are key characteristics of the Alpha Male.*

The role of the Alpha Female

Among dogs, the Alpha Male is controlled in many ways by the Alpha Female. (When this is done by a skilled Alpha Female, he is completely unaware of it.) A female dog, like a female human being, thinks *laterally* (finding connections in all directions) instead of in a *linear* way (straight ahead, moving from point A to point B, as a male does). She never directly confronts the Alpha Male dog, for she knows she would lose such a fight.

Remember this when you begin training your own Alpha Male of the human variety: The Alpha Female controls the expression of power of the Alpha Male — she modifies his natural way of moving through the world in a direct line.

> *When dogs mark their territory, they pee as high as possible (the higher the mark, the bigger the dog who made it) on the lamppost or wall, then spend quite a lot of time scratching the dirt energetically next to their urine mark. Unlike most of the dog's body, the pads of his feet sweat. The dog seeks to leave a pungent addendum to his message. It says: "Here is my smell, in case you missed my urine mark; see how long a mark I leave on the ground." Some tiny dogs like Pekingese and toy poodles, who try hard to convince everyone that they are forces to be reckoned with, will scratch a line ten feet long, moving backward to accomplish it. A Great Dane will often give just one nonchalant swipe with a back leg; he has nothing to prove.*

The Alpha Female exploits the strength and aggression of her Alpha Male for her purposes, which often center on the bearing and raising of their young. She nurtures a close and affectionate relationship with her Alpha Male. But a key point: *The Alpha Male must not be allowed to intimidate the Alpha Female, or he will not respect her.* He must be put in his proper place relative to her (which is to say he must be her equal, albeit with very different skills and a very different job to do), but she must never allow him to make her cower. There are specific things that the Alpha Female must do in order to maintain her position of equality with the Alpha Male, despite his superior physical strength. The parallels with human Alpha Males are very close. These will be examined in the coming chapters.

The wife of an Alpha Male was always assigned the job by her husband of getting the lowest airfare prices for every trip taken by their family. These trips were frequent, in order to visit his parents halfway across the country. The wife hated using computers and was not good at it, so comparing prices presented a burdensome task. In some cases it took nearly a whole day several days in a row. The Alpha Male husband questioned and critiqued her, insisting she explore every possible route to the lowest fares.

One day she told her husband, clearly and firmly, "Yes, I will take on this project and will find the lowest airfares I can. But I will assume full control of the project from beginning to end. You will have to agree to this. I will do this work my way, not yours. I am not an employee; I am your full partner in marriage. If this does not seem right to you, then please go ahead and handle the matter yourself, and I will handle a different aspect of our travel plans."

It is interesting to note that male and female brains are actually different — the *corpus callosum*, a connection between the left and right hemispheres of the brain — the 'logical' side and the 'creative' side — is far more highly developed in females than in males. So males charge ahead in a straight line, using their logical, action-oriented half, while females go back and forth using both halves to solve problems. This is actually the physical basis for the fact that females can most often juggle a number of tasks at one time, while males have trouble doing this. However, this gives males a natural edge in remaining single-minded in pursuit of a goal. Don't try to combat this instinctive behavior rooted in the male's brain physiognomy. Instead, use this knowledge to train your Alpha Male.

Men joke among themselves about "tomatoes" and "melons." Women almost never joke among themselves about "cucumbers" and "bananas."

Here is an example of the difference in thinking and behavior between an Alpha dog and an Alpha bitch; both determine what they want, but they go after it differently.

In one actual instance, the Alpha Male dog saw a bone that the female was chewing on. He wanted it. He forcibly took it away by a show of his superior strength, growling at her to indicate clearly — if she were foolish to approach him after he had taken the bone — that he (1) was in full possession of the bone, and (2) had no intention of giving it up. Alpha Male dogs, like Alpha men, are highly logical.

The Alpha bitch contemplated the situation thoughtfully for a few moments. Then she suddenly sprang to her feet, and ran barking with loud excitement to the front door, where a (nonexistent) intruder had just shown up. The Alpha Male dog raced to the front door, barking ferociously. Leaving him there to protect the house against the non-existent intruder, the female returned to the bone and quickly carried it away to a quiet spot to work on, while the male continued to guard the front door.

> *Neckties and cigars are stand-ins for male anatomical parts. An Alpha Male will poke his cigar, clenched between his teeth, in a rival's face to intimidate him. The television series* The Sopranos *shows Tony Soprano invading the space of a male adversary with a clenched cigar.*

> *Ipse Dixit*
> **ALPHA MALES IN THEIR OWN WORDS**
> *"All this Metro-sexual stuff – the 'sensitive, cultivated male' – it's really a case of just being what we think women want to see."*

In an analogous example concerning human Alpha Males and Alpha females, here are two true stories.

A middle-aged Alpha Male who is founder and owner of a successful company and is considered in his community a responsible and level-headed grown-up, was driving home after work when a young male in the car behind him leaned on the horn. Because the executive was already driving at just over the speed limit and because he recognized an insult from an inferior male when he saw one, he ignored the blast.

The younger driver then swerved out into the oncoming lane, passed the older driver, and slowed down again, clearly to 'punish' him. Moments later, the younger driver turned into the driveway of what was apparently his own house. The older Alpha Male now leaned on his own horn as he drove past to 'punish' the younger male. Whereupon, the younger driver immediately pulled out of his driveway again, pursued the car, leaned on his horn, passed, and slowed down in front all over again, an unmistakable declaration of testosterone-fueled war. The duel continued for half a mile or so before a police patrol car halted both and handed them each a summons for reckless driving.

The same thing happened to a female executive. She was passed and cut off by a young male driver who slowed down deliberately in front of her to punish her for existing on his roadway, and subsequently turned into his own driveway. The woman simply jotted down the house address, called the local police on her cell phone, reported the incident, then went home and worked peacefully on some paperwork.

The point is that what Vicki Hearne, the famous writer on dog training, calls "testosterone poisoning" lies just beneath the surface with all Alpha Males. Their behavior under stress (or when insulted) is very likely to revert to the primal battle mode. Women should remember this when they need to win a disagreement with an Alpha Male. You cannot battle against instinctive behavior if you want to win; you need to employ it for your own purposes. More about this later.

> *Ipse dixit*
> **ALPHA MALES IN THEIR OWN WORDS**
> *"We men live in a world and move through it in a stupor. Food and sex – that's truly all we see. We do not notice any nuance. We also do not listen to women. People are talking around us. We know they're speaking English, but we don't hear a word. In fact, we don't see anything either."*

Baby Alpha Males.

Alpha Males are born, not made. These true stories show typical Alpha Male behavior from a very early age.

- *A three-year-old boy was sitting on his family's front porch steps watching the 'big guys' — construction workers — digging a hole in the street in front of his house. One of the men looked at him – the child had long dark eyelashes and a bowl haircut – and said, "You're a cute little kid! Are you a little boy or a little girl?" Without hesitation the tiny Alpha Male (witnessed by several adults) replied in a piping voice: "None of your damn business!"*

- *In another case, a five-year-old boy opened the door on Halloween. Standing there was a giant in a cape with the face of Dracula above it, making the apparition nearly seven feet tall. Without hesitation, the little Alpha Male raised his wooden toy sword, at the same time spreading out his arms* *in front of his mother and six-year-old sister to force them to stand behind him, and prepared to dispatch the monster, until his grandfather pulled off his rubber mask. (An interesting side-note is that his mother and sister, without hesitating, instinctively actually <u>moved</u> <u>behind</u> this neophyte Alpha Male).*

- *Competitiveness is a key characteristic of Alpha Males. Four little boys under the age of ten were playing a game called 'High-Low Water' with their baby-sitter in their front yard on a summer's day. In the game, a piece of clothesline rope is held at each end by two people, and each child jumps over it in turn. The rope is gradually raised from a foot or so off the ground until only one child can still jump over it and is declared winner. All the children were eventually outfaced by the rope's height, which was at chest level. The Alpha Male child of the group, smaller than some of the others, stood back a moment, eyeing the rope, which was nearly as high as he was tall. Then he took a full-throttle run at it, and launched himself through the air headfirst over it.*

He landed on his hands on the other side, and stood up with bloody scrapes on both arms and a wide grin. The other boys were suitably impressed. He had won, and he kept grinning as his wounds were disinfected. He grew up to be a star high-school football player whose high scoring led his team to a state championship.

Some Alpha Males start out as juvenile delinquents. By the time they hit their teens or before, they are energetic, unruly, unmanageable by their parents. Their followers form a gang around such leaders. In many cases it is only when the young Alpha Males finally fall truly in love and marry that their energies are redirected toward protecting their family.

- *Confidence in their own judgment is also characteristic of Alpha Males from their earliest years. Two brothers, ages five and seven, were playing a game involving running, jumping, and hiding in a large playroom at the top of the house where they lived. They were having a wonderful time. Their parents, wanting to show off their children to some houseguests, climbed to the third-story playroom and knocked on the door, expecting the baby-sitter to open the door. Instead, the little Alpha Male, age five, called through the closed and latched door, "Who is it?" The mother said, "Open the door, darling. There's someone here to meet you." The small Alpha Male opened the door a crack and said, "We don't need guests," then politely but firmly closed it again.*

An Alpha Male can be truly obnoxious in his teens, at least part of the time. Studies of chimpanzee populations have been made because chimps share with humans ninety-six percent of our genetic makeup, making them closer relatives to humans than they are even to gorillas. At the equivalent age of a human teenager, the young Alpha Male chimp becomes so obnoxious that the adults throw him out of the family, and he is forced to go off and form his own family group elsewhere, in an unrelated genetic pool. This has the effect of maintaining a stronger species.

- *The parents of another small Alpha Male had just introduced their son to an overbearing baby-sitter. She was telling the child every move to make, and even at age six he was not intimidated by the large, stern-looking matron his parents had just hired. The woman said, "You will do as you are told. I am Miss Holtmeyer." The small Alpha Male was heard to say, "You're Miss Nobody to me."*

> *Princess Anne of England was shown in a videotape feeding her year-old son with a spoon. Far from telling him to eat what she was offering, with each spoonful she raised toward his mouth, she asked the baby, "Do you <u>want</u> that? Do you <u>want</u> that?" She was actively teaching him to think for himself, as a possible future Alpha Male king.*

The Alpha Male in old age or diminished health.

In old age or diminished health, an Alpha Male still retains his core qualities: He is still a winner. He still directs his full attention closely to what he is doing at the moment and moves forward in a straight line from A to B. Like dogs or wolves, human Alpha Males live in the moment, with intense focus.

The sport of *Killer Ball* — an ultra-intense form of basketball played from wheelchairs — was invented by Alpha Males who lost their legs in recent wars. If your Alpha Male is incapacitated by bad health or injury or old age, treat him exactly as you did before, but direct the action to activities he can still do. If he can't get out of bed at all, bring breakfast on a tray for you both, curl up, and ask him to tell you his war stories.

> *Ipse dixit*
> **ALPHA MALES IN THEIR OWN WORDS**
>
> *"You don't have to use a lot of noise when you've got the power of being in charge."*
> —*a Superior Court Judge*

Midlife Crisis and the Alpha Male

Many men have a rude awakening after they have spent much of their life with their nose to the grindstone, working at a job they don't particularly like but were too busy doing for all those years to really look at objectively. When such a man does step back and look at his life as a whole, he feels, to a greater or lesser degree, that he has wasted his life. Suddenly he examines where he's been and where he's going; this is a wake-up call to many men. In addition, they realize that their time left to achieve whatever they really wanted to do with their lives is short; there is no longer a sense of unlimited time stretching ahead. Some men panic. This is called a Male Midlife Crisis.

Do Alpha Males have Midlife Crises? Because Alpha Males are leaders, not followers, an Alpha Male will never remain passively at a job he dislikes (except sometimes as a calculated step in his rise upward). An Alpha Male seeks opportunity and exploits every change. He never rests until he is at the top, calling the shots for everyone else. Alpha Males are therefore nearly immune from the Male Midlife Crisis – it is more likely that they *give* the condition to a good many other males who report to them.

> *"The unexamined life is not worth living."*
> —*Socrates, in The Apologies by Plato*

A full-grown Alpha Male — who today heads his own construction company — recalls that as a child he always earned money any way he could. In Cub Scouts he took on every paying job he could find, and he had at least one or more paper routes throughout his early years. He and several other highly successful Alpha Males recently were asked what they would do if they suddenly lost all their money and their jobs. To a man, each said he would sweep streets, pump gas, or do whatever job he needed to feed his family. Not one of them said anything about welfare, government help, social security, or assistance from any other person or organization. Alpha Males nearly always work things out for themselves if they possibly can, rather than looking to others to get them out of a dilemma.

In another case, the wife of one Alpha Male is mother of a *non-Alpha Male*. This son nevertheless, thanks to his ability as a lawyer and a superior education (paid for by his Alpha Male father), gained a corporate position that pays him in the millions of dollars annually. The son is paid far more money than his Alpha Male father, yet his mother summed up the difference between her husband and son thus: "If this were 1929 all over again, and both of them had lost every cent, [my husband] would go out and get any work he could find, even digging ditches, and [my son] would be the first one out on the ledge."

A Story of an Alpha Male.

Here is a true story that illustrates the way an Alpha Male approaches a challenge.

> *In a small, quiet town, a middle-aged couple lived in a big Victorian house. The man suffered from mental unbalance. One day he became deranged and began smashing out every window of the house, using antique chairs as battering rams. Then he hurled paintings and art objects out the windows. He yelled; he smashed porcelain vases; he barricaded himself inside and continued to throw things out the windows. Neighbors gathered in the front yard to watch helplessly as he continued his rampage. His wife, watching from the front lawn, was distraught to the point of breaking. Someone telephoned the police. When they arrived, the man was still hurling objects from the third story window into the yard below. "Please stop him," his wife pleaded.*
> *"We can't do anything, ma'am," the officer replied. "Your husband may be creating havoc, but he's on his own property. We can't touch him. If he was trespassing, we could arrest him, but he's on his own property." She pleaded and begged them to do*

something, to no avail. They drove away in their squad car.

All the neighbors started giving her advice. Some advocated storming the house; others held them back, saying they could be sued for assault; others tried to yell to the man to stop; still others told them to stop yelling. The wife seemed on the point of collapse. Some neighbors had picked up as much of the debris as they could and were putting it into trash-cans that sat on the driveway separating the couple's yard from that of their neighbors.

An Alpha Male neighbor in his fifties quietly took her aside. "Wait until the crowd disperses and I will take care of it," he said.

Eventually the defenestration was complete: Her husband ran out of things to throw out the window, and the crowd gradually dispersed and went home.

Then the Alpha Male took her by the hand, walked over to one of the trash-cans full of debris, and gently tipped it over onto the neighbors' lawn. Then he called the police.

What is the force that drives the Alpha Male?

As noted, the Alpha male is driven to reach the top of any group and to lead it, to provide for it, and to protect it. He does these things without any other possibility ever occurring to him. He does this for a reason that might not seem at first logical: His behavior is based on a particular, specific kind of uneasiness so profound that it cannot be separated from his character at all. He is not consciously aware of it, but this deep-rooted uneasiness lies at the base of everything an Alpha Male does throughout his life.

Understanding how this works will give you the tools you need to marry, live with, and train your Alpha Male. Take note: Men think differently from women, and the importance of this fact must not be underestimated. Consider this all-important fact: *The male has a very limited role in the creation of young, which is obviously essential to continuance of the human species. And herein lies a primary cause of the enormous difference between the way men and women think.*

If you understand this difference and where it comes from, you can use it to modify your male's behavior and train him to be a livable companion. You will be doomed to disappointment if you attempt to force an Alpha Male to do anything he doesn't want to do. You must work *with* his hardwired instincts, not attempt to do battle with them.

All macho males are not Alpha Males. An Alpha Male always has machismo, but he doesn't always choose to show it overtly. Think of the newly rising "Godfather" in the movie of the same name, who inherits the job from his father. It is the young, careful leader, not his audacious hotheaded brother, who wins succession to be the next Godfather. The key is that the true Alpha Male is a builder. He builds his pack, then leads, protects, and provides for it. However dashing and charismatic the emotional hotheads can be, they are not Alpha Males.

Review for a moment a few obvious facts: Women carry the baby for nine months (while also doing almost all of the other chores); endure the risky and painful business of childbirth, even to the point of being carved up by well-meaning (often male) doctors in caesarian section deliveries; nurse the baby on milk produced by their own bodies; do almost all the feeding and changing and cleaning up associated with infants; teach toddlers to talk and walk; and raise, medicate, and feed children until they are old enough to do some of these things themselves. Mothers are usually the primary comforters, confidantes, and encouragers of small – and not so small – children.

Men, on the other hand, have one brief moment in procreation — their role is over almost as quickly as it begins — Blip! And they're out of there.

The Old Testament refers over and over again to 'the man who pisseth against a wall." It is clearly an important concept to the writer – if you can't piss against a wall you lack power. Dribblers aren't Alpha Males, whereas a young healthy male who can hit the wall from a yard away is likelier to be Alpha Male—and someone to be reckoned with.

Some Alpha Male dogs have actually been observed pissing higher than any other dog by taking a running leap at the wall or tree, literally running up it, and pissing away the whole time. Some of it hits very high up. ("Take that, you lesser mutts!")

Sometimes, it is true, males will lend a hand with chores and duties. But it's usually along the lines of helping with the housework by carrying out the garbage once a week, mowing the lawn, barbecuing meat outdoors on a grill, or performing a ceremonial dishwashing once a year. It is seldom the hands-on baby care like cleaning up baby diarrhea or feeding a baby who throws up on your shoulder. And if a male actually does do these things, he does them a handful of times, not the four billion times that the baby's mother does them. Further, most Alpha

Males avoid interaction with this alarming sort of work altogether if at all possible, even to the extent that some practically ignore their offspring entirely for the first months or even year or two of life.

Exceptions? Yes, of course. There are some fathers — even some Alpha Male fathers — who share equally in raising the children. But they are comparatively few. Their contribution often tends to be taking the kids out for sports or excursions. Women still perform almost all the housework and have practically the sole role in bearing and rearing children. No man, of course, can do anything that even comes close to the all-encompassing, intimate connection with children of mothers, who nurture the child for nine months prior to birth, and then literally bring the baby into the world.

Ipse Dixit
ALPHA MALES IN THEIR OWN WORDS

"Men are interested in perpetuating the species. Men don't like children who aren't their own. They want to perpetuate the species with their own offspring, but really don't care a whole lot about other people's offspring. They actually don't care as much about perpetuating the species as they care about perpetuating their own seed.

"A lot of Alpha Males can be in a relationship with a woman but have issues if she has a child by another man, whereas a woman is more often willing to walk into a circumstance where the man has a child by another woman."

Because of their awareness of their tenuous place in the process of creating children, literally a piece of themselves to go into the future, Alpha Males spend a great deal of time posturing. When courting, they strut, puff up, flex their biceps, brag to and show off in front of women. An Alpha Male does this to impress a choice woman and make her believe that he is powerful enough to feed her while she is carrying their young, and protect her while she is nursing and raising the children. He seeks to convince her that he is a strong, healthy example of the species with whom she should breed in order to have healthy, strong offspring.

> *While he is supremely confident in all areas of his life that rely on strength, intelligence, swiftness, or perseverance, an Alpha Male's life is in fact resting on quicksand. There is an insecurity that dwells in the very core of the Alpha Male's being. This insecurity, which is as inseparable from the male as the very breath he takes, must be properly handled by the woman planning to make a life partner of an Alpha Male.*
>
> *He knows instinctively that his role in the continuation of the species can easily be replicated by some other male unless he stands eternally watchful. If this were to happen, the unbroken line of reproduction that began at the dawn of time millions of years ago (or with Adam and Eve, depending on whom you ask) will end, truncated and cut off forever with his own life, thus ending with this particular male who is trying hard (albeit unconsciously) not to become extinct. This makes men very uneasy at a deep subliminal level.*

Later he postures in order to drive away any other males who may be circling the camp. And while doing all this, the Alpha Male is simultaneously driven to gain through his own efforts a good place to live with his mate and family, and a good income to provide for them. It is a very heavy workload; only the strong survive.

Most males don't articulate this uneasiness in words, or even see it clearly or consciously. But it serves to keep the protective, providing Alpha Male almost continually on guard, in a state of medium-to-high alert, ready to vanquish any other male who dares to come close to his group. The thought of raising another man's child when he has been duped into thinking it is his own is anathema.

Little or none of this is conscious, of course. Alpha Males can't help this behavior; it is the way they are constructed. The urge to reproduce is, after the drive for food, the strongest driving force in almost all males. The Alpha Male is just that much more driven in this respect than the rest.

According to Konrad Lorenz in his book On Aggression *most animals establish dominance by ritualized posturing, feints, and body moves intended to frighten but not actually harm adversaries. This is the way most animals establish hierarchy. The ritual showed a clear winner and a loser; the loser skulked off, defeated and humiliated. As one writer asked in a review of the book, "Isn't it possible that, absent the power of guns, humans could reach the same level of civilized behavior as the other animals?"*

It is fundamentally for this reason alone that Alpha Males behave the way they do, which is the subject of this book. And, since males still pretty much control the workplace, this information spills out into that subject as well, and will be explained in future chapters.

<u>Training a happy and contented Alpha Male.</u>

A happy Alpha Male will be a good provider if his mate makes him feel loved, cherished, admired, and respected for what *he* wants to be respected for. To make an Alpha Male feel diminished and uncertain about his role as protector and provider is to destroy his feelings of leadership and to shake his confidence to the core. The Alpha Male needs every bit of confidence he can muster to go out into a dangerous and hostile world every day and do battle on behalf of his woman and children. He is driven, relentlessly, to succeed; he cannot accept failure. An Alpha Male might rightly say: "I'm doing my part (lead, protect, and provide). Why aren't you doing *your* part (organize a peaceful safe haven where I can retreat between battles with the world to protect you and our pack)?" This drive to succeed at all cost, coupled with his essential drives to lead, provide and protect, makes for an exhausting life unless he can retreat from time to time into his safe haven — his well-ordered place with mate and children. His survival, and therefore that of his pack, depends on his being able to regain his strength between battles.

Here is a heretical thought: *No woman should expect an Alpha Male to share in most of the chores needed to run a house.* This is because an Alpha Male made to do menial chores becomes less important in his own eyes. No longer a warrior, he feels himself diminished into a janitor or trash man (perfectly honorable occupations in themselves, but almost no Alpha Male wants to be one, unless the idea is entirely his own and he himself *chooses* to do it. If so, the chore assumes a separate status: It is now acceptable work like anything else he has himself chosen to do).

An Alpha Male should be nurtured, even coddled, at home so he can recharge his engine. If you expect him to do much more than that, you can destroy his sense of self. He needs this in order to go out each day and fight for his pack.

There are ways to get a fairer distribution of chores, but tread carefully. Women who want to hold onto an Alpha Male but don't like being stuck with all the menial tasks should learn to approach the matter obliquely, not head-on. The ways to do this will be explained in coming chapters. There are tools to use so you don't become the sole drudge doing household chores. But nagging, begging, or confronting won't work.

> *An Alpha Male will be better pleased by your comment that you're impressed by his ability to lift up the garbage cans two at a time than if you tell him how tidy he is for not spilling orange peels on the driveway.*

It is for this reason you don't expect an Alpha Male to help you box up your parents' belongings when they sell their house, or to dig out the trash in the basement of your house, to change the baby's diapers, or to discuss with you your innermost insecure feelings or worries. The Alpha Male must think of himself as a leader able to take on the world and to win, each and every time. If you attempt to force him to take on other roles, you demoralize him, weaken his resolve, and make him deeply unhappy. Although he probably will not say in words what is bothering him, it will come out in some other way – anger, silence, or absence.

> *Ipse Dixit*
> **ALPHA MALES IN THEIR OWN WORDS**
>
> *"A lot of things that women would like to have males do, like changing diapers, like making the bed—men don't actually care if it happens at all. There are two levels to it. It's not just that they don't want to do the work; they don't care if the work gets done. Does the trash have to get taken out? Not really..."*

Is an Alpha Male right for you?

Get your sights set on what you want. If you are interested in finding a life partner who is a good provider, a courageous companion, protective, an exciting and interesting counterpart *very* different from yourself — this book will tell you how to go about acquiring and training your own Alpha Male.

If, on the other hand, you find yourself gnashing your teeth at this line-up of qualities, or if you want a male with whom you can share your every inner feeling, you'd be well advised to consider whether you really want to team up with an Alpha Male in the first place.

As noted, Alpha Males do certain things supremely well, but they do *not* do certain other things well, or even at all. They require careful and consistent training and handling. This is not to say that a woman who is herself competitive and driven cannot have a very good life with an Alpha Male — *as long as she is not competitive with him.* As long as her drive is directed outward in some other direction – toward her job for example – a positively thrilling partnership between an Alpha Female and an Alpha Male is possible. But certain very specific things are required to make such a partnership work. These are discussed in the following chapters.

2.

FINDING AN ALPHA MALE

How do you find an Alpha Male? And what do you do to attract him? In this chapter you will learn the best places to find an Alpha Male. You will discover how to get him to notice you, and what to say — and *not* say — once you engage him in conversation. You will also learn how to get him to follow up with a second meeting. The chapter also tells you twelve of the things that attract men most in a woman.

Where can you find an Alpha Male?

The best places to meet Alpha Males are *not*, surprisingly, at sporting events like football games and ice hockey matches. The action at events like these is too intense, and the Alpha Male's attention will be riveted to the sport.

Further, whenever there are a number of Alpha Males in close proximity to each other, there is a type of male competitiveness that takes over. They show off for each other (as male wolves or dogs do by posturing and strutting around and scratching the dirt; human Alpha Males at sporting events yell, punch each other, and spill things). They won't have any attention left to direct toward you.

Remember that nearly all males can only follow one line of thought or action at a time — they go from A to B to C. Lateral thinking is difficult, and multitasking is alien to them. Look for your Alpha Male in a locale where he will be able to notice you and apply his single-minded attention to you, not a sporting event.

Although the best places to locate Alpha Males require a less fast-paced atmosphere, they definitely include places that are *related to* sports of different kinds. Here are some of the places to try:

- Attend *automobile shows*, especially those having to do with antique cars and sports cars (an outstanding Alpha Male husband today was first spotted looking at vintage trucks).

- Go to *military museums* and attend *military commemorations and events.* Officers have had rigorous training to command men, and they don't usually become officers unless they have strong leadership qualities.

- Attend *working-dog field trials* (Labrador retrievers, beagles, sheepdogs, Scottish deerhounds, etc.) Also go to *police dog exhibitions.* Ask the American Kennel Club in New York City or search on the Web for information on locating events.

- Go to *lectures on sports subjects.* Libraries can sometimes tell you of upcoming speakers on subjects from baseball to scuba diving.

- Join a *speakers' bureau.* One of the best types is a speakers' bureau featuring experts on *world affairs.* These tend to attract intelligent men (and have resulted in some highly successful marriages). Google 'speakers' bureau,' 'world affairs,' and the city nearest you.

- *Church.* You don't of course attend for the purpose of meeting Alpha Males, but the fact is that many such men attend church regularly. Volunteer to work on a committee for a church supper or project.

- *Genealogical meetings* can be worth canvassing, if you happen to belong to a genealogical organization. Figure out if you are descended from somebody interesting (virtually everyone is, if you dig a bit) and check out a society that applies — Descendants of Civil War Veterans, for instance, or Veterans of Foreign Wars, or Descendants of the Signers of the Declaration of Independence, or any of scores of other organizations. Take a look at the *Encyclopedia of Associations* (online or in any library) for ideas.

- If you happen to live in or near New York City, have breakfast at one of the coffee shops in the vicinity of Wall Street. You'll be surrounded by traders and by stockbrokers, who are very often Alpha Males. Have a woman friend with you and a copy of *The Wall Street Journal* to study and discuss. (It may be interesting to go to the visitors' gallery and watch the action on the trading floor after the bell rings in the morning).

- *College and university clubs* exist in most cities. If you are a graduate or have a woman friend who is, go to lunch or attend events.

- *Skeet-shooting events.* "Clay pigeons" are small disks launched into the air as targets. Consider taking up sport shooting yourself. It doesn't hurt animals, and it's fun. There are lots of Alpha Males who skeet shoot.

- Spend a day or two at a *trade show for inventors and entrepreneurs with new products.* Entrepreneurs are very often Alpha Males. Many are quite approachable and ready to talk at trade shows.

- *White-water river rafting,* especially in magnificent country like Wyoming or Colorado, by definition has Alpha Males (or sometimes Alpha Females) leading the adventure. Ask a travel agent or check online for rafting trips.

- *Skiing* is one of the best ways to meet Alpha Males. The instructors are almost always Alpha Males, as are the ski patrol. If you don't know how to ski, take group lessons (you could meet an Alpha Male in the class). Once you're a decent skier, you can ski a run with a man (up on a lift together, where you have a chance to talk, then ski to the base of the mountain), and if you don't especially want to continue that association, choose a different prospect and ski a run with him.

- Work as a *volunteer on a political campaign.* The atmosphere is hectic and friendly; it's easy to talk with fellow supporters of the candidate; and because it's voluntary the rules against dating where you work do not apply (see Chapter Nine).

- *Volunteer to wash airplanes at your local airport.* You can sometimes do this at small airports; hanging around the hangar you will meet many Alpha Males who own their own airplanes or are taking lessons or working on their instrument ratings. If you can afford it, take lessons yourself. Many instructors fly company jets for large corporations and teach flying to the public in their off-hours; some are not married and most are almost certainly Alpha Males.

- If you live near the water, get a *part-time job at a yacht club or marina* scrubbing the hulls of boats and washing decks. Or start your own summer business delivering coffee and bagels via dinghy to the moored boats in the harbor. Many Alpha Males skipper their own boats. Many are single. Some of them have made single-handed crossings of the Atlantic and may be looking for a first mate.

- *The gym or fitness club.* Enroll yourself in a fitness program, and you can see the Alpha Males at work on one of their favorite occupations: building their strength. You can increase your own fitness, and if you are in good shape already, Alpha Males will notice.

- *College reunions.* Some classmates who were married may have now lost their wives; some who have never married may now be interested in finding a wife. Among most college classes are at least a few Alpha Males.

- *Blind dates.* Women have met their Alpha Male husbands on blind dates they didn't think would be worth the effort to get ready for. Always consider the possibility of a lucky introduction.

- *Parties.* These can sometimes lead to meeting an Alpha Male, although it depends on who is giving the party and what kind of friends they have. If you do notice someone you are interested in, follow the steps outlined in Chapter Three.

- *Weddings.* You already have a slight connection with any Alpha Male you may spot at a wedding — you both know either the bride or the groom. The subject of lasting union and happiness through marriage is very much in the air at a wedding, which works in your favor.

What about your chances of finding an Alpha Male in some of the *least likely* places? (Notice how often humor plays a part.)

Here is a list of some *unlikely* places where some women did, in fact, meet their Alpha Male husbands-to-be. These should not be considered necessarily advisable ways to meet Alpha Males, but they do illustrate the point that you never can tell when or where you may meet someone who will prove to be the Alpha Male you've been looking for:

- *Walking the dog.* Her Chihuahua attacked his Labrador retriever; the dogs got into a fight; the Chihuahua had to be taken to the veterinarian (the Labrador only had sore ankles). The Alpha Male drove her to the vet, and later took her to dinner. He also paid the vet bill (the Chihuahua recovered). They married a year later; both dogs were present.

- *Stepping off a curb into traffic.* He grabbed her by the arm and prevented her from getting hit by a car coming from the wrong direction. Then he asked her out. (Do not attempt to duplicate this way of meeting!)

- *Garbage-truck worker* had a sign on the vehicle that said '*Your Satisfaction Guaranteed or Double Your Garbage Back.*' She laughed at the sign; they started talking. He was a candidate for public office and was doing a stint at a manual job to get a genuine feel for how hard blue-collar work can be. (He had invented the sign for the truck and was pleased she had thought it funny.)

- *In a grocery store.* She was taking advantage of a sale on paper goods and had filled her cart to the top with toilet paper rolls. He was in line behind her at the checkout counter. He looked at her quizzically for a moment and asked, "Are you expecting a *crisis*?" She choked laughing; he fell in love with her on the spot.

- *Charity event volunteer.* She was a volunteer food server at a high-ticket charity event intended to raise money for the homeless in a large city. A man, whose wife was out of town, had come with his visiting Alpha Male cousin as his guest. The cousin had just raised a spoonful of soup to his mouth when someone jostled his elbow, pouring the soup down his tie and shirtfront. Without thinking, she remarked, "Everything you eat looks good on you." He stared, and burst out laughing. He stayed in touch when he returned to his home city, they later dated, and they were married a year and a half later.

- *On the subway.* It lurched; *he* landed in *her* lap. He told her he almost *never* sat in women's laps, but the least she could do was return the favor, and would she consider it at some time in the future? No? Then what about lunch? (She took his business card, left her work phone number a day or two later, and they had lunch the following week.)

- *At a bar.* Bars attract habitual drinkers, losers, liars, men who cheat on their wives, and drunks. The inebriating effects of alcohol do not work to promote honest conversation or bring out most people's best qualities. Bars are among the *worst* places to find an Alpha Male. However, good men, Alpha Males among them, do go to bars on occasion, and some women have indeed met their Alpha Male husbands at bars. But you should put bars as absolute last on your list of places to look for an Alpha Male. They are almost always simply a waste of time. Choose a bar that serves steak.

Your strategy for meeting an Alpha Male for the first time: some important dos and don'ts

A word of advice before you set out to find your Alpha Male: *Always take a woman friend along with you.*

Don't choose a woman friend who is less pretty than you are. Go with someone you genuinely like, and the better-looking, the better. Agree ahead of time what your game-plan is, and at some point return the favor by helping her in the same way if she wants you to. (Incidentally, an Alpha Male often marries the woman who is *not* the most beautiful, but *who makes him fall in love with her.* How you do this is a learnable skill, which will be explained in detail.)

There are several reasons for going with a woman friend. One of the most important is that a friend gives you 'third party endorsement,' which simply means that because you have a friend with you, the Alpha Male can see that you are liked and accepted by at least one other person. This is important when making the first step to meeting an Alpha Male. These men are leaders, men who make choices and then act on their decisions. They do not feel comfortable being 'led' anywhere, even into conversation. (The only exceptions to this will come much later, when he is completely in love with you and trusts you — then he will welcome your taking charge of certain aspects of his life.).

But especially at the outset, Alpha Males want to initiate things, and then make absolutely *all* the moves forward thereafter. A single woman is a possible trap for him — what if he wants to get away but can't politely leave her standing all by herself? What if she's completely alone because she is a neurotic lunatic and has no friends? With your friend standing by, questions like these don't arise.

Second, you can show a bit of who you are to the Alpha Male without actually acknowledging him. That is, with another woman you can appear to remain completely oblivious to the Alpha Male while engaging in conversation with each other; you can laugh, smile, walk around, comment to each other about what you are doing or seeing, and place yourselves strategically where you wish (in his line of view) without its appearing forced. If you are a woman alone, you cannot easily do this. This brings us to a very important point.

Why must an Alpha Male notice you first?

The reason you do not acknowledge the Alpha Male at first is simple. You must give him plenty of time to look you over and decide himself that he is interested in finding out about you. You need to give him the opportunity and time to notice you and decide he likes what he sees, *without any pressure to do or say anything*. This is the first step in training him to pursue you. It is an essential step.

> *His first impression of you imprints on his memory. It will never change. Make sure it's a good one.*

Don't worry, if he is interested, he will approach you. *This stage is critically important.*

> *"Man chases woman until she catches him."*
> *—Old saying*

You may be tempted to think, "I'll just smile at him, or go over and ask him a question because he seems too reserved to approach me." *Wrong!* The Alpha Male must believe he controls the action from the very beginning. *He must always pursue —* otherwise he will feel he is not in control, and will have a deep-seated fear that he may be sucked into something he will have trouble extricating himself from later on. Because Alpha Males must always win (or die trying) they are careful about getting into situations in which they feel control will be in someone else's hands.

At this stage, your job is to attract the Alpha Male, nothing more. To do this, behave in a way that would make you attractive as a life partner. That is, no silly girl-giggles or overblown gestures or actions. Just dress and look your best, focus your *full* attention on the exhibition or whatever you are looking at or doing. You and your woman friend should talk quietly, but with animation and a spark of fire, as long as it isn't forced.

You should give the impression of being completely absorbed in what you are doing, and having a very good time doing it. Nothing attracts other people as much as a person who is obviously happy and having a good time. Place yourselves in his line of vision, move around from place to place if it makes sense to do so (as you might, for instance, at an antique car show, keeping your attention on the cars). Don't so much as glance at him.

<u>Meeting an Alpha Male for the first time at a party.</u>

Let's say you have gone to a party and have noticed a highly attractive Alpha Male prospect. Women are all sidling up to him and batting their eyes and trying to engage him in conversation. What should you do?

When you first walk into a party, stand for a long moment and look all around the roomful of people in a general way with your most brilliant smile. Look dazzlingly happy to be there. This says to everyone who sees you, "I'm friendly and I'm happy to be here, I'm approachable."

Do not get a drink yourself, so that a man can approach you later by offering to bring you one. Then make your way slowly with your woman friend to a spot about four or five feet away from the Alpha Male if the room is crowded; a longer distance if there are fewer people. Don't look directly at him, but be certain you are directly in his line of sight. Proceed to carry on an animated conversation with your friend; it can be about anything at all (but make it clear you are not discussing any of the other guests). Stand so you are partly turned toward the Alpha Male, but not facing him directly.

If another woman or a man of any age or appearance approaches you, engage the person in conversation and make him or her feel welcome. Smile, nod slowly as the other person speaks, keep eye contact, laugh at the jokes, and tap a man's arm — between wrist and elbow, anywhere else is considered too personal — as though to 'punish' him for telling such a funny joke. This gesture creates an immediate connection with him. Even if he's not the one you want to attract, the Alpha Male will notice the fact that people are drawn to you and have a good time in your company. If others join the group, so much the better. Have fun and let it show. This won't go unnoticed. The Alpha Male may after a time 'cut in' and offer you a drink. Or he may simply bide his time.

Never discourage *anyone* from coming up to you and speaking with you, even if you are only interested in meeting that one Alpha Male you've noticed across the room. Not only is it rude and hurtful, it makes you look snobbish and unfriendly; the Alpha Male who watches you do this to another man will be far less likely to take a chance of having you snub him. Welcome *all* who approach, and use the occasion to practice your skill of making conversation exciting and fun for all participants. In any case, sometimes a man you weren't initially attracted to turns out to be truly terrific, and you can make new women friends at parties, too.

If the Alpha Male hasn't approached within ten minutes or so, you and your woman friend should say what fun it's been talking with the others in the group that has formed around you, and drift off to say hello to someone else. If the Alpha Male has become intrigued with you, he will follow you sooner or later and initiate a conversation.

<u>What to say when the Alpha Male you are interested in initiates a conversation.</u>

First, greet his approach with your most glorious smile. Then proceed to get him to do ninety to ninety-five percent of the talking. Focus your full attention on him. Do almost exactly what you would do when you meet a seven-or-eight-year-old boy: Talk facts and numbers. That is, do not ask "How are you?" or other personal questions. Small boys like conversations that deal immediately with facts, like "I know how to teach a dog to go down a sliding board," or "I can whistle so loud that if I show you, you'll have to hold both hands over your ears."

Grown-up males are very like small boys — at a first meeting they are much more comfortable talking about subjects that have little to do with them personally. Go armed with some interesting facts and statistics, such as: "I've just learned that three out of every ten people who attend opera regularly are avid baseball fans. I wonder why that is?" or "There are thirty-two sunken boats per square mile in the Bermuda Triangle. How do those pirates get away with it, I wonder?" or "If you make a stack of large-denomination bills worth one *million* dollars, it's six inches high; A stack equaling a *billion* dollars is as high as the Washington Monument, five-hundred feet. A stack totaling a *trillion* dollars would be ninety-five *miles* high. I never could get my mind around those numbers until I read about how high the stacks of money were."

The Alpha Male will probably ask where you got your information; a conversation is off and running.

How to carry on a conversation with an Alpha Male.

After a few moments of general facts / statistics conversation (during which your woman friend slips away for a drink or to say hello to someone else, leaving you alone with the Alpha Male), ask your first real question. From this moment on until you leave him, focus your entire attention on him; ignore anything and anyone else in the room.

Your questions will take on a form that is probably different from anything you've ever done before upon meeting a man for the first time. The pattern is: Ask about his childhood, not his present life. This will surprise him and it will connect him to you in a way he has not connected with anyone else. All those other women hanging on him were asking about his career and present life, or were trying to tell him about themselves. You are entirely different.

Ask him questions like these: "How old were you when you had your first job? What was it? Did you have other jobs as a kid?

Which did you like best? What did you like best about that job?" Ask gently and don't rush from one question to the next. He shouldn't feel he is being grilled. Take your time. Show your reaction by nodding, laughing or smiling when warranted, and make the occasional noncommittal comment like, "Yes, I can see how you might say that," or "That must have been fun," or "What a difficult thing that must have been." Don't offer your own opinions or views on anything at this point. Simply get him to tell you all about his.

Think of it this way: Pretend to yourself that you must go home and write a full report of this man's early life from, say, ages six through ten. Ask about his parents, his brothers and sisters, his likes and dislikes, his early school, his pets, sports he liked and didn't like, his introduction to computers and whether he liked them from the start or not, his summer jobs, his camp, people he hated, when he learned to swim, how he got to school (walk? bus? bike?), whether he ice-skated on a pond or at a rink, who his favorite people were outside of his family, what his favorite music was, what his mother was like, if he sang at school or in a choir or played a musical instrument, what his favorite foods were, and anything else that will bring up memories of his earliest years.

Don't rush him. Don't make it seem as if you have a list you intend to cover. Just keep the questions in the back of your mind and let the conversation flow. It doesn't matter if he answers all the questions — and if he goes off on a tangent, so much the better.

What you are actually doing by this line of discussion is threefold: First, you are getting him to do almost all of the talking; he should be doing ninety to ninety-five percent of it.

Second, you are learning about him in a far more useful way than you would by asking him about his present life. Adults learn to be guarded; children usually are not. By remembering his life at that time, he is giving you an unguarded glimpse of the man he is today.

Third, you are beginning to seem very, very different from most other women whom he meets, who discuss their jobs, their hobbies, people they know, what they do, and where they go, and who do most of the talking.

> *"The child is father of the man..."*
> *—William P. Wordsworth*

If he asks you a question, answer as briefly as possible without seeming to give a short answer, then ask him another question about his childhood. For instance, if he says, "You're asking about when *I* was a kid — well, how about *you*? What was *your* life like at that age?" you might answer, "Oh, fun! My sisters and I got into trouble as often as possible. We once went on every ride at Disney World twice and forgot our parents had said to meet them at eight p.m. When they arrived at midnight in the company of two large police officers we were *quite* surprised. But you were telling me about how your brother and you built a go-cart and entered a soapbox derby against bigger kids. That must have been fun! Was there a prize? Did you win? How did you build it?" etc.

At some point he is almost certain to stop you and ask, "Why do you want to know all this stuff about my childhood, anyway?" Simply say, "You are an extremely interesting man, clearly a leader and not a follower, and you have a number of other qualities I've observed that make you very different from other men. I just wonder how you got that way." He will not be put off by this answer, and may become more intrigued. Then ask him another question about his childhood years. If he presses for specifics you have noticed about his (present-day) qualities, tell him something like, "We'll get to that. Right now, I want to know how you built the soapbox go-cart. Please tell me about...."

<u>Setting the stage for the Alpha Male to pursue you.</u>

Suppose the above conversation took place at a party: After about eight or ten minutes, not longer (*especially* if you're enjoying talking to him a great deal), tell him, "You are a *fascinating* man. I've *really* enjoyed talking with you! I've got to go say hello to some friends now. I'd like so much if we can talk more later, I *really do* hope so."

Give him a wide-eyed, genuine smile holding his gaze for two or three seconds, then make your way to another group, or find your woman friend. Don't be lured into staying too long; leave him now, and *set the stage for him to pursue you, not vice versa.* Due to the nature of your conversation with him, he absolutely will not forget you. If he asks for your telephone number, *tell him you'd like his business card and say you'll leave your number on his voice mail or email in a day or two.* Then be sure to follow through, leaving your business number, *not* your home or cell phone number.

<u>What to do if he *doesn't* follow up.</u>

First, here's a list of things never to do: *Do not call him, email him, send him letters, or in any way pursue him.* It's the kiss of death to life with an Alpha Male. Yes, some women have pursued men and eventually married them; however, if a man is an Alpha Male he will be very wary of being pursued, and marriages that result from entrapment are often just that: traps.

What *can* you do? Discreetly find out whether you have any friends in common. If so, get one of them to have a dinner party, invite you both, and seat him directly across the table from you (*not* next to you; it is not as easy to talk and he cannot look at you as easily). Or, if he said anything in his conversation that gave you an idea of places he frequents, whether at work or in off-hours, consider showing up 'by chance' one time more.

If he's interested, he'll make sure to show it. If he sees you and does nothing to follow up, forget it. There is nothing — repeat, *nothing* — to be gained by trying to pursue an Alpha Male. Your goal is to make a true match, not to attempt to force an impossible pairing-up. Both sides have to be attracted. The reasons a man responds to a particular woman are complex, having to do with any number of factors in his present and past life. If the relationship doesn't start to sail along fairly easily, you must move on without delay.

<u>Twelve of the things that attract men most: A checklist.</u>

These may be obvious, but it's worth reminding yourself of them:

- *A fabulous, genuine, dazzling smile.* It tells people "I'm glad to be here; I'm open to meeting you; I don't need anything from you; I am fun to be around."

- *Clothes that are freshly laundered, fit well, and make you look good,* whether jeans that show off your curves or a dress that makes your legs and figure look terrific.

- *Clean, fresh-smelling hair.* Many men prefer the scent of just-washed hair to scent of any kind.

- *High energy.* You don't want to express your energy by racing around pointlessly, which merely looks frenetic. Energy can be expressed in quieter ways: It makes your eyes sparkle; it makes you quick to pick up on what someone has said, or to laugh at a joke made by someone else. It is evident in your body language, even if you're standing still. It makes you aware of others, which is flattering to them.

- *Dressing in a way that is sexy without being obvious.* Show off your back instead of your cleavage, or choose a long dress that shows one leg with a long slit cut to mid-thigh.

The back of your neck, your shoulders, your collarbone are also sexy. So are feet in high heels.

- *A graceful way of moving.* Observe how certain people walk, sit, stand, run, or turn to look at something. Copy the ones you like.

- *Confidence of manner.* This can be convincingly imitated even if you don't always feel it. Practice the appearance, and eventually it becomes an actuality.

- *Eye contact.* Make the person you are speaking with feel he or she is the only person in the entire world you have any interest in at that moment.

- *Makeup that enhances* enough to bring out your best features and minimizes any you don't like. A light touch, not a theatrical overdose of lipstick, mascara, or powder.

- *Very high heels* — only worn in suitable places, of course. Many men are turned on by them. (Be sure to practice before appearing in public on four-inch spikes, however!)

- *A beautiful speaking voice.* Not only the words you use, but also the quality of the sound itself. Speak slowly; keep the register low. Avoid high-pitched or rapid speech. Have a genuine, whole-hearted laugh, not a girlish titter.

- *Friendliness to other people.* Everyone responds to this. Consideration of other people is always attractive — not obsequious or fawning, but forthright, kindly interest in other people is one of the keys to being genuinely liked by both men and women.

<u>What to do when he asks for your telephone number or email address.</u>

Let's assume that the Alpha Male you have met has shown interest in taking things a step further. He's asked for your telephone number or email address. You *don't* give it to him yet; instead, you ask him for *his* business card. You tell him you will leave your number on his voice-mail or his email; this makes him wait and think about you for a bit, and you don't appear too eager, which starts it off right: He'll have to pursue you.

You follow through as promised — you put on his phone mail or email your work number, not your home or cell number, a couple of days later. He calls you (immediately or the next day or a week later) and asks you to meet him for a drink the next night after work.

How you handle the dating process with an Alpha Male is the subject of the next chapter.

<u>It worked for them: True stories of women who attracted Alpha Males they later married.</u>

- *At a party, a woman who saw a man she desperately wanted to meet went up to him and said, "Will you do me a tremendous favor? I have to go speak to someone, but will you <u>promise</u> to come and rescue me in <u>exactly three minutes</u>?" She gave him her first name only; they synchronized watches.*

  She then crossed the room and approached the handsomest man at the party, who was surrounded by women. She asked him about someone she said she thought he knew. He gave her his full attention (trying to figure out to whom she was referring). In exactly three minutes, the man she was interested in came over and said her name. She turned to him, rewarded him with a dazzling smile, excused herself to the other man, and went off with the man who had 'rescued' her. (It was not until years after they were married that she told him of her ruse.)

- *Another woman used to frequent the local bookstore. She would leaf slowly through the pages of a book, standing near a man she wanted to meet. She would then 'accidentally' drop a book and some papers of her own. Then she would get down on her knees to collect them, looking up at the man while doing so. The man invariably helped her. She met her husband this way.*

- *Another woman watched a game of men's lacrosse. They won the game. As the Alpha Male she was interested in walked off the field, she said to him, "I'll bet I can tell you three things about you when you were a little boy. First, you never, <u>never</u> gave up. Second, you were a leader from when you were very little. Third — no, never mind about that." He demanded to know — she hedged and said it might take some explaining. He of course asked her to meet him for a date. When they met later that week she explained that he was clearly an Alpha Male, and how, and why. They were married in less than two years.*

Are tricks like these fair?

> *"All's fair in love and war."*
> *—Old proverb*

3.

DATING
AN ALPHA MALE

How do you date an Alpha Male? Here, in detail, is the "game plan" that sets the stage for getting this highly attractive Alpha Male to begin to see you as different — and far more interesting than any other women he has known. You'll learn what to talk about on your first date, some pitfalls to avoid, and secrets that are little known even to some very savvy women.

The action so far.

You've got his attention. He's met you at a party or an event of some sort; he noticed you and you talked with him for eight to ten minutes (you made sure he did ninety percent or more of the talking). You kept the entire conversation focused on his early childhood years. When ten minutes were up, you let him know you find him fascinating and unlike any other men. You've told him you hope very much to talk with him more. Then you floated away from him, just out of reach.

He asked for your home or cell phone number; you said, "Why don't you give me your business card instead?" and told him you'd put your number on his voice-mail or email in a day or two. You did so, leaving your work phone number. The stage is set: You are friendly, but ever-so-slightly elusive.

Now he has called you at work — can you meet him tonight for a drink after work?

You're elated. What should you say to this highly attractive guy whom you really, *really* want to know better?

If he asks you out for the same day, the next day, or the day after that, what you invariably say is: "I *wish* I could! I *really* enjoyed meeting you. It's impossible right now — I'm booked solid until (name a day four days later). There's *so much* more I want to know about you".

He'll be surprised, because these highly attractive Alpha Males don't get turned down very often. On the contrary, most women pursue *them*. But he'll be intrigued. Either he'll ask you on the spot for a date later in the week, or he'll think about you for a while and call back with an invitation for a few days later.

Should you make yourself "available"?

Always stick to this rule: *Being "available" is not the way to his heart.* Make him think you are unavailable much of the time, and that *he can only pin you down by pursuing you.* The key to it is to be warm and enthusiastic whenever he calls; just don't make yourself too readily available. Make him wait and think about you. Always let it be known you have lots of interesting things going on in your life, which is the reason you can't accept his invitation until at least three or four days later. Do not be specific about just what all these other commitments are if he asks. Just say something vague like, "Oh, you know, friends with a boat," or "It's too complicated to go into right now, but I will say this — it will be really fun if it's not too scary." Don't let him drag anything more out of you. Just laugh and say, "Well, I do have some pretty interesting friends, and they always seem to be cooking up these incredible adventures."

<u>When your Alpha Male calls back and asks you out three or four days hence.</u>

> *He's only sure of himself while pursuing. The reason? Pursuit is akin to sex; he can't perform if intimidated. Pursuit of himself by a female frightens a male: What if he gets caught and then can't perform?*

He calls back and asks you for a date for dinner the following week. You say something along these lines: "Thanks! I'd absolutely *love* to have dinner with you!" Unless it makes no sense logistically for him to come and pick you up, tell him where he should come for you. However, if picking you up at your home would create a logistical nightmare, suggest you meet at the restaurant. (He should, however, see you home to your door but not inside.)

Plan ahead to look your best. Be well rested if you can. If you drink lots of water for at least a day before the date, your face will have an attractive glow (the water washes toxins out of your system, and hydrates skin cells). Use a light hand on makeup. Dress simply and look your stunning best.

Do not so much as offer to pay *any* part of the costs of the evening. He is an Alpha Male: He leads, provides, protects. This is his nature. If he doesn't do these things, he doesn't feel he is in charge. When the check comes, say something like, "Thanks so much; that was really lovely."

After several dates, if you decide you like him and want to continue to get to know him, you can reciprocate in other ways such as cooking for him, taking him on a picnic, organizing a special event to which you invite him as your guest, and so on. This will be covered in detail later. But let him ask you out at least three or four times before you reciprocate.

<u>What to talk about on your first date with an Alpha Male.</u>

The answer is simple: Talk about him, for almost all of the date. That means you must ask him questions and listen carefully to his answers, which will influence how you ask the next question. It must not sound like an interrogation; rather, you should be friendly, easy-going, and ready to smile and laugh when warranted.

If he asks you about yourself, answer pleasantly but briefly, and go back to asking him about himself as soon as you can.

But don't lose sight of your goal: to find out as much as possible about him. You will use this information for two purposes:

First: To set yourself apart, in his eyes, from all other women he has dated (who routinely talk about themselves as much or more than they ask about him). Second: To determine, after enough information is asked, whether his goals and values are enough like yours for a successful marriage.

Try to keep a level head — Alpha Males all have that wildly attractive, magnetic quality of energy and purpose about them. But if your goal is a lifetime of successful marriage to an Alpha Male, you will be well advised *not* to fall head-over-heels in love with him. *In fact, it is critically important that you do not fall in love with him, at least until after he is fully committed to you.* Fall '*in like*' with him for now, but not '*in love.*' What you must do is *make him fall in love with you.* This is possible to do; it is a learned skill, which will be explained in detail in this and following chapters.

You must not fall in love with an Alpha Male until he is in love with you. Your job is to make him fall in love with you. This is a learned skill.

So, know in advance that your first date (and those that follow) will be made up of gentle questioning with the purpose of getting an Alpha Male — many of whom do not talk easily until they begin to trust you — to talk about himself to you.

Your goal at this point is to listen attentively and with approval, refrain from voicing your own opinions, and encourage your Alpha Male to unfold the story of his earliest years from childhood up to and including high school. These are the years which formed his character, his preferences, his likes and dislikes, and developed his strengths; in which he learned to hide or camouflage his weaknesses from other males, and essentially became the man he is today. If you can understand his unguarded young years, you can understand him today. Even if he is a highly successful man at the top of his game, inside he is still the same boy you are learning about by your gentle, approving questioning.

Why should your questioning be approving and not critical?

At this stage, if you show disapproval — even slightly — you will drive him away. He will feel he has shown you his vulnerabilities by revealing his early years to you, and if you disapprove, he will feel betrayed.

Later on, when a good solid bedrock of trust has been built, you will be able to do several things you must *not* do at this point — these include telling him about yourself and giving constructive criticism (that is, you will not tear him down personally, but you will say in what way you think *his behavior* is wrong — that is, incidentally, the *only* kind of criticism you should ever give). And, similarly, you will in the future discuss topics you must avoid for now — sex being the most obvious. Why this is so will be explained in detail later.

Who? What? Where? When? Why? How?

Begin your questions with one of these key words as often as you can. (These key words are used by journalists who interview people for articles or news reports.) They encourage the person being questioned to answer expansively rather than in one or two words. For instance, if you ask: "Did you like sports from a very young age?" the answer may be "Yes." But if you ask, "What kinds of sports did you like best when you were very young?" the answer will probably be much longer and more revealing.

As before, start by asking him about his childhood followed by years up to and including high school. Don't stick rigidly to a list of questions; it doesn't matter if he talks about his early years, then jumps to high-school years, goes back to early years and so forth. The important thing is to keep him thinking back and sharing his reminiscences with you. Depending on how much of this he already discussed with you when you first met him, elicit answers to questions like these:

- *Firsts*: Bike; friend (male) and friend (female); fight; job; trip; summer camp; success; failure; achievement in sports; school prize; pet. Earliest memory; first time away from home; first major loss.

- *Favorite:* Teacher; mentor; sibling; friend; grandparent; school subject; animal; clothing; food; book; television show; movie; music.

- *Activities*: Was he in the Boy Scouts or in a 4-H? Was he in a club? Was he a member of *Mensa* (people with high IQs)? Did he work on the school newspaper? What things did he join, and what did he like and not like about each?

- *Most disliked*: Teacher; friend; food; chore. Whenever you can, find out why he felt this or that way about something.

- *Money*: Allowance; after-school job; summer job; gift money. Did he save his money? Spend it? What did he spend it on? Would he do the same again? Did he envy kids with more money than he had? Did he look down on kids who had less? Were his parents proud of him for earning money? If he'd won a thousand dollars as a kid, what would he have done with it? What if he'd won a lot of money while in high school?

- *Family*: Favorite times; least favorite times; where he lived; what it was like growing up in that house / apartment / condominium / farm; what his hometown was like; how he views his own childhood. Would he want his own kids to have a similar upbringing? Don't ask this question directly, because you want to keep his focus on his childhood, but take note of what he says and how he says it. How is his relationship to his sisters? To his mother? To his father? His brothers?

- *High School*: What were his friends like — the guys he hung out with and guys he respected? Which teachers he respected and why. When he first got interested in girls. Which girls he dated and which girls he wished he had dated — and what he liked and didn't like about them. His first car; favorite sports; academic achievements; extracurricular activities; hobbies; after-school and summer jobs. What was his happiest moment? His most embarrassing moment? His most frustrating moment? What made him most angry? What he was best at? Worst at? What would he do differently if he could? What would he do exactly the same if he could? What did he look like in high school?

- *Special training*: Wilderness survival; piano lessons; science club; fire fighting; CPR; dog training; ballroom dancing; rifle shooting; or other? What did he spend time learning? What did he wish he had learned, and why?

These are just some of the kinds of questions you want to have ready for your first date. Don't under any circumstances refer to a list. Just keep the questions in mind in a general way.

Stay away from questions about sex for the time being. These questions will come later, when there is trust and understanding between you. Asking too soon puts the focus on the subject, and it will take over and completely block out all other considerations and memories. Sex is an extremely important subject to most males, and to Alpha Males in particular.

Your aim for now is *to make sure your Alpha Male has a very good time talking to you.* He will, if you ask the questions in an unpressured, friendly way, and then listen attentively to all his answers. He should be the entire focus of the evening. He should feel as if, to you, he is the only person in the world while he is talking. If you glance over his shoulder even once at another male, he can feel you are not really interested in him and clam up.

Is this work? Yes. But since you are discussing the life of the Alpha Male with whom you are at least potentially considering spending the rest of your life in marriage, it is well worth the effort.

<u>Your game plan for the present: A reminder.</u>

- Remain slightly elusive by not being available when he snaps his fingers — make him wait to spend time with you by accepting dates only if they are scheduled three or four days or longer after he asks you.

- Be ever-so-slightly mysterious — you do this by asking him about *his* life — beginning with his formative childhood and young years. You always keep the focus on him. For the time being, you learn a great deal about him, but he learns almost nothing about you, apart from the fact that you look great, have a nice way of speaking, and are very, very much interested in his life and how he became the Alpha Male that he is now — different from any male you have known besides him.

- Be warm, friendly, and kind. Be uncritical of him for now — constructive criticism comes later.

- Allude to a private life of your own that is fun and exciting, without letting him in on the details.

- Look and sound your best — attract him, and get him to pursue you; *never* pursue him.

- Begin by asking about his childhood and early years up to and including high school.

Is this manipulation?

Yes, absolutely. At this point, you are trying to make your chosen Alpha Male *do* certain things: talk to you and reveal his unguarded character to you, and begin to see that you are very different from any other woman he has ever dated. You are also trying to *prevent him from doing* other things: becoming distrustful, rejecting you, or walking away. Manipulation, which means in general, 'moving someone or something around for a purpose,' is not in itself a bad thing. It matters how you do it, and what your purpose is.

You must, without question, play fair. His trust in answering your questions must never be betrayed, compromised, or used against him in any way — during an argument, for instance, or in anger. You do not ever have the right to use against him later anything told you now.

For a marriage to work really well, you must treat him with respect from the very first day you meet, and throughout your marriage (if you decide to marry him). He must of course treat you with complete respect as well — and how you teach him to do this is the subject of future chapters.

4.

HOW TO MAKE AN ALPHA MALE FALL IN LOVE WITH YOU

Now to the nuts and bolts: How can you make an Alpha Male fall in love with you? Believe it or not, this is a learned skill, which you can use over and over if need be until you find the Alpha Male you want to marry. There is a secret to making an Alpha Male fall truly in love with you and see you as different from every other woman he has known. (This secret explains why great guys often fall for selfish, 'bitchy' women.) You'll also learn how to address the question of sex and how to handle it with your Alpha Male. The answer to this question is likely to surprise you.

<u>Why some terrific men fall for bitchy women.</u>

Why do some of the nicest, most worthwhile women never get proposals, while some selfish 'bitchy' women get lots of proposals? Why do some very average women who are not particularly good-looking, and even, sometimes, not particularly nice, end up with absolutely terrific husbands, while some very nice women are passed by?

Some of the most attractive men (a group that includes most Alpha Males in their number) fall in love with and marry quite ordinary-seeming women. These women are not necessarily the most beautiful — or even in some cases particularly pretty. They don't have to be the most stylish or have perfect figures. On occasion, they are not even particularly nice. Yet their husbands are obviously happy and content with them; in some cases, they still appear to be head-over-heels in love after decades of marriage. If you think about couples you know, or even observe certain married couples in public, you will see that this is true. What accounts for it?

The answer is surprisingly simple:

The woman who acts aloof or bitchy (tells him off, shoves him away verbally, generally disagrees with whatever he says and frequently puts him down, but also intermittently is exceptionally sweet to him) can appear to an Alpha Male to be sure of herself and therefore superior in some way.

He thinks, in his *linear*, male way of thinking: "If she is so aloof and has such high self-esteem, and considers herself too good for most men, she must be superior to other women. If she is willing to let *me* chase and perhaps catch her, *I must be better than all those other guys."*

(Note: This pattern of thought bears startling resemblance to another pattern of Alpha Male thinking described later in this chapter — that is, the question of how males feel about women who sleep with them before marriage — *it has more to do with how they think of themselves than it has to do with the woman.)*

> *Remember that all males love to measure things all the time, and one of their favorite things to measure is themselves.*

The drawback to becoming a bitchy woman yourself is that, sooner or later, many Alpha Males wake up to the fact that the woman they thought so superior at first really isn't what she pretends to be, and that the much nicer woman they noticed later is a lot more fun to be around.

> *Unlike a man, a woman observing another woman who is bitchy and aloof might, in her female, _lateral_ way think: "I wonder why she considers herself so much better than anyone else? Is she overcompensating for some sort of insecurity? Has she just shown up in the city from a small town and feels out of place and therefore acts prickly to hide her uneasiness? Is she trying to prove something to someone else in the room? Did she miss out on learning good manners at home? Does she know her slip is showing?"*

The key is to maintain your own sense of self. You must never confuse 'being nice' with being a doormat. Many genuinely nice women make this mistake. You need to maintain your own integrity, and make him *respect* as well as love you. You can have high self-esteem without being a bitch. *There are specific things you can do and say that will accomplish this.* How you do this is discussed in upcoming chapters.

Yet how did bitchy women — as well as nicer ones — end up with great husbands?

These women all knew the secret of how to make their man fall in love with them and stay in love with them. Some absorbed this know-how from watching their mothers, who were in good marriages to their fathers. Some learned what to do by watching the bad marriage of their parents and determining to do things differently and much, much better. Some had mentors who helped them; some had the help of good women friends; some had a good psychologist; some read books and put what they learned to work.

It doesn't matter at all how the knowledge is acquired. But good — even great — marriages don't 'just happen.'

Having in-depth knowledge of how Alpha Males think and act gives you a powerful, nearly foolproof tool for making men fall in love with you. (It also creates a profound responsibility not to

> *In every case, good marriages require a good match of the two halves. That is, both sides believe that they got a very special person. And each person likes and admires the qualities in the other person that that person likes best about himself or herself.*

misuse the tool.) The end result will be to convince him you are superior to any other woman he has ever met, to make him see that you enhance his life without cramping his Alpha Male style, and that you understand him as no other woman has ever done.

One of the ways you begin to do this is by taking on some, but not all, the tasks you will probably handle in the future as his wife.

Entertaining your Alpha Male: Two key areas where you should take charge.

By this time, you will have spent perhaps twenty to forty hours in the company of your Alpha Male. When he takes you out, he pays. You do not ever offer to pay even a part of the cost. It is the job of the Alpha Male to provide — this is natural to Alpha Males. *You are training him to think of you as someone he provides for.*

However, you do, of course, need to reciprocate. What you do depends on your talents and abilities. The two most important things you should do for your Alpha Male are: first, *feed him,* and second, *begin to take over running the aspects of his life that he is not good at.* The most obvious area to organize is his *social life* — going to dinner, seeing friends, attending parties, and the like — almost everything, in fact, other than his work.

By doing these two things, you make him comfortable and simplify his life; he can concentrate on excelling at work, which is what Alpha Males do best. He will begin to notice that you 'fit' into his life, and that things run more smoothly because of you. Far from hemming him in, you expand his reach.

- *Feeding the Alpha Male*: By all means cook for him if you are a good cook. If you are so good at it that you can talk at the same time as you work, let him sit at the kitchen table while you whip up something delicious. He will associate the good, homey smells of food and the satisfying meals with you.

> *"The way to a man's heart is through his stomach."*
> —*Old saying*

If you do not cook, or do it badly, bring in the food already prepared and put it on your own plates. Or take him on a picnic (find out his favorite foods and drink ahead of time). Or plan impromptu adventures where you end up eating with chopsticks from a Chinese take-out box while sitting on park benches. It doesn't matter what you do, so long as you keep it interesting, slightly unpredictable, and the food itself is good. He will grow to rely on you for making his life interesting and effortless and fun.

- *Social life*: Once in a while, get tickets to some event you know he will enjoy. If he's an ice hockey fan, spring for the best seats you can get. If he loves classical music, take him to the performance of a renowned violinist.

If money is in short supply, take him to *just one* event and do it right (the best seats, the best event). He will remember it. Let the rest of the entertainments you plan for him cost little or nothing. Sometimes a long walk along an empty beach in winter can be as much fun as the most expensive outing. Whatever you choose to do, handle all the details and planning.

What you should be talking about at this point in the relationship.

At this point in your relationship you can begin asking your Alpha Male about the future and the present. But don't be in a hurry. The progression should be gradual and natural.

- *Asking about the future.* When you finish learning about his early life, for the next several times you are together, ask him about his future — what he will choose to do in his working life in the next year, the next five or ten years; where he'd like to travel; what interesting things he'd like to do (Build a log cabin in the mountains? Go fly fishing in Argentina? Bicycle across the United States? Open a general store? Grow rare plants? Build an organ? Fly to Alaska to watch the *Iiterod* sled-dog races?) Does he intend to earn a lot of money? Does he want to have a family at some point? What does he most look forward to in the future? What does he most want to have happen?

- *Asking about the present.* When you have spent several days or weeks learning about his hopes and dreams for the future, ask about the present: his job; his commitments to parents and siblings; his interests; his friends; his enemies; his concerns; what he finds funny; what he says makes him angry; his views on loyalty; his views on money; his obligations, financial or otherwise; his religious beliefs; whom he admires or respects and whom he doesn't; his political views; his world view; whether he likes children; whether he likes pets; what he considers the perfect vacation; whom among his married friends he thinks has the best life.

But there is one highly important subject that will get his full attention and make him feel that you, above all other women, truly understand him and what he is about. With the proper groundwork laid already, this will bring his emotional commitment to you to a new level.

The key to making an Alpha Male fall in love with you.

The final component to making an Alpha Male — whose nature is to lead, provide, and protect — fall in love with you is this: You ask him questions about himself that are central to his nature and character: *In other words, you ask him about what makes him an Alpha Male* (without asking the question directly).

When he digs deep to articulate his most essential Alpha Male characteristics — which he may never have voiced to anyone else in his life before because no one knew how to ask the questions — *he will feel that you understand him as no one else ever has. This is the secret of causing him to begin to fall in love with you.*

> *"You don't buy a car when you see one you like, or when the salesman tells you all its great features. You tell him what's important to you, and you buy when you feel you've been understood."*
> *— The leading car salesman for Mercedes-Benz*

If you understand him as no one else does, approve of him, look good, are pleasant to listen to, are kind and considerate of him and other people, and are quite obviously very, very much interested in him (although *not*, at this stage, obviously 'in love' with him) why in the world would he *not* fall in love with you?

Thirty-four questions to ask your Alpha Male that go to the heart of what makes him an Alpha Male.

As before, when you questioned him about his early, future, and present life, do not make this sound like an inquisition or an interrogation. The questions are best put very gently, in conversation, with no hint that they have come from any list. It may take many talks over weeks or longer to get answers to them all. Take it slowly and encourage him to talk about anything else he wants. Do not discourage diversions of topic; let him digress as much as he will. Then merely return, presently, to another question. Use this list as a guide:

- When did you realize that other guys took their lead from you?

- What is the bravest thing you ever did?

- Did you ever protect anyone from bullies?

- Did you ever protect anyone from danger?

- How old were you when you realized you were a leader, not a follower?

- What did you do in your life that makes you most proud?

- At what age did you know you would be a success?

- How did you choose your field of work?

- What was your father like when you were growing up?

- Are you like your father?

- Who are your heroes in history?

- What has made you really angry?

- What has ever made you afraid?

- How did you act courageously when afraid?

- Would anything other than dishonor stop you from achieving your goals?

- Have women always pursued you?

- What do you most respect in other men?

- What is your most cherished memory of, or favorite quality about your mother?

- If you were in high school again, would you do anything differently?

- If you were in college again, would you do anything differently?

- If you were determining your career again, would you do anything differently?

- Can you imagine or 'see' a picture of how you want your life to go from this point forward? What would you like it to be like in a few years?

- Who was your best buddy growing up?

- What was the most fun you ever had together?

- What was the scariest thing you ever did?

- What is the most important thing you have ever done?

- What is the second most important thing?

- On a scale of one (least) to ten (most) how important to you is winning whatever battles you choose to engage in?

- On a scale of one to ten, how important is freedom to become all you want to become?

- On a scale of one to ten, how important is loyalty to you?

- If you could change places for twenty-four hours with someone and live his life, whose would you choose?

- What are the most important achievements you want to accomplish in your lifetime?

- Which *one* achievement would you say if you could only choose one?

- Are you aware that you are an Alpha Male?

Note: Do not ask him what qualities he wants in his ideal woman — it is too obvious that you are asking for yourself, and he probably will merely tell you what he thinks you want to hear. Instead, ask him what he admires most about his mother, sister, or other female relative or friend.

<u>Sex before marriage — an ironclad rule you must never break, and the surprising reason behind it (you may be shocked).</u>

When you get to the point where you are comfortable enough to ask — and your Alpha Male is comfortable enough with you to answer — these core questions about what makes him the Alpha

Male he is, it's time to deal with the question of sex before marriage.

Sex is extremely important to Alpha Males. Besides the strong interest in it that virtually all males have, Alpha Males have an additional, extra drive to excel and succeed and win. This means they feel a compelling need to find and capture and win for their own the *very best* female. (If you've forgotten how it works, go back to earlier chapters and review how Alpha dogs and Alpha wolves do the same thing).

> *"Why buy a cow when milk is so cheap?"*
> *—Old saying*

The reason not to have sex before marriage has almost nothing to do with you. It is almost entirely a question of how the Alpha Male sees himself. It is all about the Alpha Male.

Why is it so important to remember this point? Because it becomes increasingly hard to resist an Alpha Male, who is undeniably attractive (often devastatingly so) who is clearly attracted to you, with whom you share a good deal already, and with whom you are growing more certain all the time that you want to spend the rest of your life. It can seem almost absurd to resist the strong urge you both have to consummate the marriage before any vows are made.

But this is exactly what you must do if you want to marry this man and have the highest level of respect and love from him for the rest of your life together. Yes, people do violate the 'no-sex-before-marriage' rule all the time, and many people think it 'safer' to try out sex together before the marriage commitment is formally made. Many people think it advisable to live with the man you intend to marry and do a 'trial marriage' with the possibility of simply walking away if things don't work out. Undoubtedly, some good marriages come out of such cases.

But here, from an Alpha Male point of view, is why you should not have sex with your Alpha Male until you are, in fact, married to him.

Here's what he will think, the morning after — he will almost certainly *not* think these thoughts consciously, and may be almost unaware of them even if you asked him directly. But the fact remains, these feelings will stay with him, and will color, either to a lesser or greater degree depending on many other circumstances, the rest of your life together. They may only come out in the future some time, such as during the heat of an argument over something trivial.

What he will feel is this:

"I am an Alpha Male. I am the leader of the pack — so it is my right to have the best job, the best way of life, the best of everything because I am the top dog.

"I demand a female partner who is equally top-choice. She is so desirable and so elusive that only a male as great as I am — an undisputed Alpha Male pack leader — could ever get her to be my partner.

"We slept together and it was great. I really do love her. But, *since I was able to sleep with her without marrying her, so could a lesser male.* Therefore she is not as top-choice as I originally thought she was.

"And, therefore, since all I got was a not-quite-top-choice woman, *I am not as great as I thought I was."*

This makes the Alpha Male feel less powerful, less potent, less in charge of his life, less a leader, somehow diminished. This feeling may be slight, it may be unacknowledged, it may never be voiced, but it will be there. *Because the Alpha Male feels diminished in his own eyes, however slightly, he will regard you with slightly less respect, even if you do in fact later marry.*

But you will have lost one of your most valuable and potent tools: his absolute conviction that you are the best female in existence *since he is the only male in the entire world to have won you in marriage, and subsequently, the only one able to sleep with you.*

Do not underestimate the importance of this to an Alpha Male. It goes right to the center of his being. If an Alpha Male does not feel 'full of himself' and proud of who and what he is, he cannot function fully. If there is a chink in his armor, other males will sense his vulnerability and try to exploit it and destroy him. The world in which he works is hostile, with the exception of the safe haven his wife can provide; this is the one place, the only place where he can let his guard down.

By sleeping with him prematurely, you have taken away a little of his self-confidence and strength. Some men, after sleeping with a woman, even a woman they like a lot, will simply drop her and never see her again. No explanation is given; they just stop calling. They aren't 'using' her — she went into the deal with her eyes open. They just can't stand how vulnerable it makes them feel the next morning.

(This will not, however, prevent your Alpha Male from asking or even pressuring you on the question of premarital sex).

How to answer when he wants to sleep with you (before marriage)

Even if you have had 'a past' with other men, decide from the beginning that you will refrain from having sex before marriage with a man you want to marry.

What if he says he really loves you, and he just can't go on 'being friends' without having sex with you? You tell him: "Every man I've ever dated wanted me to go to bed with him. I think far too much of myself for that. I'm special. I'm not like all the other women you've dated. *Do you think I don't know* how fantastic sex with you would be? It's *really hard* to hold myself back with a man like you, because you're so different from any man I have ever known."

Tell him you are *extremely* attracted to him, that he is nearly impossible to resist, but that you cannot be considered in the same category as other women.

Say, "Sex isn't hard to find in today's world. For someone as great-looking and sexy as you, all you need to do is stand still and you'll be surrounded by women throwing themselves at you for sex.

"But what *I* am and what *I* have to give is *very* hard to find. I believe in myself. I'm better and I'm not ordinary. And I am looking for a lot more than unattached sex, even with someone I'm as greatly attracted to as I am to you.   And anyhow, once I let myself loose with a man as attractive and sexy as you, I couldn't control myself. I might just go wildly out of control for the rest of my life. I can't take that risk."

If he keeps insisting, repeat variations on the same theme until he stops. Don't expect him to be happy about it; he won't. But it won't kill him, either.

Needless to say, it is unwise to put yourself into situations where it will be difficult to extricate yourself. Don't entertain him in your bedroom for example. Keep your aim on the long term goal: a happy marriage lasting many years to an Alpha Male, with whom you will share complete trust, loyalty, respect, and sex as well as love.

<u>An Alpha Male tells how his future wife attracted him.</u>

"I am at a cocktail party at the home of a friend. For some time, I have been looking for a woman to marry. Across the crowded room is a bunch of single woman of the right age, chatting together, none of whom I

know. I immediately see the one woman in the group I am interested in.

"She is stunning, in an elegant, understated sort of way. She is feminine, but not overly so. She has some curves, but not of the Bimbo (enhanced) variety. Her clothes are tailored and fashionable, but not cutting-edge. They definitely are <u>not</u> revealing — no 'meat market' for her. She looks successful: no very-long hair (gets in the way at work); no Mandarin fingernails (how could she use her hands on the job?); no gargantuan earrings (how could she talk on the phone?). She wears a single strand of pearls. She's got class.

"She stands straight, head high. She has good eye contact. When engaged in conversation, she is all attention. She listens more than she talks. When she smiles — and she is not always smiling — it is an open, full, sincere smile with sparkling eyes. And she can laugh; she radiates warmth.

"She is probably wearing makeup, but not a Kabuki mask. Nothing you can notice, anyway. No blue eye shadow, no exaggerated eyelashes or purple lipstick — I am looking for a wife, after all, not an opera diva.

"She does not chatter. Her voice is soft and sure, but when she speaks, I notice that the other women listen. She exudes self-confidence. She shows no evident interest in the men sniffing around her. Most of them realize they are out-classed and haven't got up the courage to approach her.

"Casually, I walk across the room (every man in the room is watching) and introduce myself."

<u>When should you turn a man loose who is not a true candidate for marriage?</u>

What should you do when you have dated a man for a while and still aren't sure you want to marry him? Use the *Three-Month Rule: If you aren't sure after three months, turn him loose.* When you begin to date a man you like, give it three months and then decide to go on if you want to marry him, or stop seeing him if you don't.

The reason women get confused by a man with good qualities, who is nevertheless *not* the right man for marriage, is this: We think, "He has these good qualities. Therefore I *should* love him and want to marry him. Those nagging doubts I have about certain *other* traits he has that make me uncomfortable or that I don't like (even if I can't put my finger on exactly what they are) must be figments of my imagination, because he does have all those *other good* qualities..."—and the argument goes round and round in a circle and gets nowhere.

Realize when he is *not* the right man for you, despite his many good qualities, and send him off for another woman to find who is looking for someone exactly like him. Don't spend time making allowances for his shortcomings or overlooking traits or patterns of behavior that make you uncomfortable or upset or even angry. Cut him loose and move on.

Above all, *don't think for an instant that you can marry him and then change him. You can't.*

All of the men who will become interested in you are not genuine Alpha Males. Some may want *you* to lead; some may even want you to provide most of the income; some men really do want to be house-husbands. There is nothing wrong with choosing to marry a non-Alpha Male if you both want this.

There are myriad reasons that can cause a relationship to founder. When things aren't working, when things aren't getting better and better, easier and more comfortable day by day between you, he is not the right man to marry.

Many of us waste days, months, even years, trying to force a match with someone we should have let go long ago. We feel it is somehow *our* fault; that if we just try harder or make this or that adjustment, the whole relationship will improve. Don't all relationships have rough patches where things go wrong? Of course. But the general trend should be that it gets better as time goes on, not worse. If this isn't the case within three months, it should be pretty clear. If he *is* the right one, it will become increasingly clear to you that there is no one else you can imagine being with for the rest of your life.

How should you break it off?

Some women choose just to become less and less available until the man gets the idea — they think this is kinder than telling him outright that while they like him, he is not the right potential lifetime partner for them.

It is fairer, however, to explain the situation with absolute clarity so he will realize that you have thought carefully about it, have made a definite decision and that there is no point in his hanging around trying to make you change your mind.

Tell him (if it is true) that you have many women friends who would be very happy to meet him, and follow up by introducing him to friends. (He may be too angry to accept this, however.) But leave no doubt that you are ending the relationship. It is unfair to keep anyone on a string harboring the unrealistic hope that you may change your mind in the future.

Above all, do not 'settle' for a man who is less than what you really want. If a man isn't exactly right, try for three months. Then move on and keep looking. The right man is waiting to be found.

The rule is: Keep looking until you find exactly the man you want to be married to.

5.

GETTING
AN ALPHA MALE
TO PROPOSE MARRIAGE

Now you have an Alpha Male who is in love with you. How should you begin to make yourself essential to him — and what tactics should you use to make sure he realizes that you are?

Following the steps shown here, you can train your Alpha Male to seek your approval — and eventually to propose marriage.

This chapter also reveals the three key reasons men don't propose, and what you can do to trigger a proposal (yes, this *can* be done, with some regularity, if you know how).

<u>Train your Alpha Male to seek your approval.</u>

He initiates; you give encouragement and your warm approval. He pursues; you are welcoming, but always that little bit elusive, so he pursues again and again. He always gets his reward, your warm response, but when you are far enough along in the relationship — when it is clear that the two of you are serious about one another and heading toward a full-time commitment — it is time to *withhold approval for things you disagree with or don't like.* This withholding is *never* an attack on him personally, on who or what he is. Rather, it is *correction of behavior* either that is unfair to you, or that makes him appear vulnerable to the enemy.

Who is the enemy? Everyone outside the Alpha Male's pack (those he protects and provides for, plus any male friends who, by mutual consent, have laid down their arms and struck a friendly, if on occasion rivalrous, truce.) The Alpha Male seeks a partner who is one hundred percent loyal to the pack, just as he is — who will stand with him against the whole world if need be.

<u>Why your Alpha Male will actually welcome your corrections.</u>

It must be repeated: *Never make a personal attack on him, his beliefs, his family, or friends. Make a correction of behavior,* which is a very different thing.

Let's say you are both at dinner at the house of some friends. The host is going on and on about something, and he has his facts wrong. Your Alpha Male, showing off just a little, tells him just how and why he is wrong. It embarrasses your host, and his wife is embarrassed for her husband.

First, and very important, *never correct him even a little bit when anyone else is nearby.* For the moment, just change the subject. Wait until you are entirely alone, preferably after he has had something to eat (less likely to be cranky). *Never critique his words or actions in front of others, even if you are angry.* This is the beginning of the end of a good relationship, as it will break his trust in you.

For instance, a *personal attack* by you on your Alpha Male would go something like this: "You always try to undermine other people and you are always shooting your mouth off." (This belittles him and shows contempt for him.)

A *correction* (for the same offense) would be: "It hurts people's feelings if they are criticized, especially in front of their friends. Would you be willing to try just letting them rattle on with their own ideas, however stupid, rather than setting the record straight when their families are listening? I want the Joneses to like us — and anyhow, you surely know that *I know* you are much smarter than he is." (This merely points out a cause-and-effect, and asks an adjustment of action by him.)

Your Alpha Male will welcome your corrections, if done tactfully and in private, because he will realize that you are not out to harm him or diminish him; on the contrary, by the manner and timing of your corrections, it will be clear that you are speaking to him about a wrong action so that by correcting it, he will correct a weakness and thereby strengthen himself and his pack.

As he grows to trust you, he will count on you to provide this 'extra set of eyes and ears' which act on his behalf and that of his pack, and he will know that you are loyal to him, care about him, and can be counted on to have his best interests in mind.

All this should happen without your ever having to say verbally, "I really care about you" or "I'm really on your side." Alpha Males, being men of action themselves, are much more likely to believe actions than words.

Why men don't propose marriage.

The reasons men do not propose marriage, even when they are in love with a woman, could be summed up in many cases by three words: *Money, Freedom,* and *Youth.*

- <u>Money — the first reason men don't propose.</u>

Financial concerns can make any man, especially an Alpha Male, wary of getting in over his head. If he considers you a wild spender, a person careless with money, or someone who will try to influence him toward spending money in ways he would not spend it himself, it can make him pull up short and never ask you to marry him.

The unknown is the biggest cause of his fear — that is, his not being sure how you regard the money he earns now and will earn in the future. Remember that *for Alpha Males, money equals power*; the more you have, the bigger and more formidable you are. It is deeply important to him that you, as part of his pack, will help him in his acquisition of power and money, not fritter it away behind his back. This doesn't necessarily mean he will expect you to *earn* money — many Alpha Males are spectacularly good earners and really only want your praise and admiration for this ability — but he will want you to help him by standing with him on how money is spent.

> *For Alpha Males, money equals power. The more money you have, the bigger a man you are.*

Therefore, you need to show your Alpha Male, from the start, that you are responsible with money and conscious of how hard anyone must work for it. Let's assume that you are, in fact, a person who is reasonably careful about money. You have a job or career; you pay your rent or a mortgage; you may be repaying a loan for education; you pay for your own clothes, food, travel, and so forth. It is quite easy to drop into your conversation once in a while a comment about the satisfaction you feel in being able to do these things, and the knowledge you have, from working, about how hard it is to earn money. Your Alpha Male may not say anything when you tell him this, but he will most certainly take note of what you said.

Because Alpha Males are always focused on succeeding, and any woman who can support herself is a success, he will know that your views on money have at least some common ground with his own. *He himself has no other option than to earn money; no self-respecting Alpha Male would dream of living off his wife's money.* Because he is an Alpha Male, he must earn enough for not only himself but for his 'pack' — those he supports and protects.

If you show him that your views and training as regards money are similar to his own, you will remove one of the most critical points of uncertainty that can inhibit or prevent him from proposing marriage to you. Your Alpha Male should know that when he earns money for both of you (and a family later on, as well as perhaps for others like older parents), you will be squarely in his corner, helping him to conserve it and use it wisely.

- Freedom — the second reason men don't propose.

An Alpha Male grows up making his own decisions from a very early age. Of course his parents control most of his actions early on, but even from childhood he is thinking his own thoughts and taking his own course of action wherever he can.

As a boy and as a young man he is already a leader. He assesses situations and acts; other males follow his lead. When he reaches manhood, he has grown into his potential. Almost no one and nothing can stop him once he sets his course, unless he chooses to change course. *His freedom to choose what to do and when to do it in every aspect of his life is central to his being.*

An Alpha Male fears losing his freedom, and this can make him wary of proposing marriage for fear that once married, his life will change in ways that are at present unspecified but will forever prevent him from being what he is: a leader. He will find it difficult or even impossible to put these fears into words.

Therefore, they take on even greater importance, because they do not get brought out into the open and discussed.

> *In America today, it is fashionable to say that all men's clubs should be open to women and that all colleges, including women's colleges, should be made coed.*
>
> *Some disagree: The National Survey of Student Engagement sampled more than forty-two thousand students at nearly three hundred four-year colleges, both coed and women's. They determined that graduates of women's colleges constitute more than twenty percent of women in Congress and made up nearly a third of the "rising women stars of business" as listed in <u>Business Week</u> magazine. The study concluded that in many respects "women's colleges are models of effective educational practice and have much to teach other types of colleges and universities."*
>
> *There is a case to be made that a need exists for organizations that admit only men, or only women. Many Alpha Males really enjoy the company of other males, away from the need to be on their best behavior around women.*

You cannot confine a true Alpha Male to a set of circumstances that curtail his actions. He is what he is. He must remain free to act. (You can, and should, *train* him, however; the difference is that with training, he learns to cooperate and to respect you and your point of view even when it differs from his own — more about this in upcoming chapters).

You can begin to put his mind at ease about the question of freedom by *alluding to it* rather than trying to discuss it directly. To be too direct is to make him admit he has fear, which alone will make an Alpha Male uncomfortable. (Much of an Alpha Male's time and effort is spent in convincing the world at large, and other males in particular, that he is fearless and a man to be reckoned with.)

You could, for instance, ask him about trips he has taken as a young man with his male friends. Maybe he took a backpacking or mountaineering trip, or a canoe or rafting trip. Maybe he and a buddy or two worked as ski bums for a winter. By asking him about such adventures with his male friends, and listening attentively and approvingly, you can then say something like, "Those times with your friends have a really special place in your life, don't they? I'm sure you will never want to lose the freedom to do things with your buddies." Just a throwaway line like this will indicate to him that perhaps less will change than he feared if he asks you to marry him.

- Youth — the third reason men don't propose.

Youth seems as if it will go on forever when you are young. Then suddenly it's over, and you are expected to become responsible.

Of course this is an illusion. The Alpha Male who has made no lasting commitment by the time he is grown will find his friends have nearly all married or made lasting commitments of their own. Far from being carefree, he will find himself alone and somehow outside the action. But a rosy glow lingers in his mind about the years of his life before he was expected to do much more than show up and have a good time with his friends. (This too is an illusion; there were always responsibilities, but he remembers the irresponsible parts best because they were the most fun.)

So the Alpha Male fears proposing marriage because it will *effectively end his illusion of still being young and carefree.* He knows at some level that it isn't true, by the time he hits is mid-twenties or so, but there is something so final about actually getting married that makes him hesitate.

Make it easier for him by saying, from time to time, something like, "You look so much like a teenager when you throw that ball. I guess there are some things you never lose, once you know how." Ask him what some of the things are that he'd most enjoy doing if he had the time and money. Get him to remember what he liked best as a boy and as a young man. Let him see that many of these same things are still possible, and let him know that to you he seems a young man when he does them. You can't give him back his youth, but you can help him enjoy remembering it, and he will associate this enjoyment with you. This will help ease his fear of losing his youth.

Three trigger words that help a man propose marriage: (Hint: It is _not_ "Love," it is _not_ "Care," it is _not_ "Forever.")

The three trigger words that can spur a man to actually propose marriage are: _You, Freedom,_ and _Choose._

Here is why:

Marriage threatens to make him less able to do whatever he wants whenever he wants. He fears this. He fears being diminished, 'lost' in the marriage, merely half of a twosome, no longer the potent Alpha Male.

- Every time you say _you_ he knows he is in the center of your attention. He knows that you are interested in who he is, and in what he wants. Talking about his early years, then about what he wants in the future, and finally about his present life, puts him squarely in the center and shows him that you consider him important.

- Using the word _freedom_ reminds him that you don't intend to cage him in or restrict him from being who he is. Just the word itself goes a long way toward creating an atmosphere in which he will feel he can continue to be himself, with the added advantage that he now has your approval and support.

- Use the word _choose_ in general conversation with your Alpha Male. Instead of saying "What are you going to do?"

ask: "What will you *choose* to do?" Using the word often indicates that you consider him a leader and that you understand how his mind works. If Alpha Males don't lead, they are very unhappy men. If he sees that you expect him to choose how he lives his life, it will remove another impediment to his asking you to marry him.

If he hasn't proposed within six months.

Choose your moment: Wait until you have both had a particularly good time together. Give no warning of what you are about to say. Then take his hand, look him in the eyes, and tell him, "I have to say good-bye to you now. I have decided to go my own way. It is true we always have a wonderful time together, and you already know how much I admire and respect you, and what I feel for you. I think we make a really great team, in fact. But I'm a woman who wants a great deal more than this. I need the *full commitment* of someone as terrific as you. Since it doesn't seem that we are going in that direction, it's time for me to move on. Good-bye."

Then walk out the door without looking back.

Give him a couple of weeks to come to his senses and realize he is losing you forever. If that realization doesn't hit him squarely between the eyes (in which case he will ask you to meet him and will propose on the spot), then he doesn't deserve you.

In such cases, he isn't the right man and you cannot make him the right man no matter what you attempt. (You will be glad, in this case, that you did not sleep with him.) You may be tempted to try to lure him back by some strategy. Do not attempt this because you will be doomed to disappointment. If things don't work out, put it behind you and renew your search to find the right man. A perfect match for you is looking for you this very moment.

But if he is really all that you believe him to be, he most certainly will not let you get away. He will propose.

Proposals of marriage by the Alpha Male.

Nearly every fairy tale (a very old story form going back many hundreds or perhaps even thousands of years) that included a Prince wooing a Princess followed the same formula: First he observed her, and then he fell in love with her. Before he could marry her, however, there were always three next-to-impossible feats he had to accomplish. These generally included slaying of dragons or scaling of walls or outwitting some enemy or other. Then, and only then, could he win the hand of the Princess in marriage.

These Princes were all Alpha Males. They were brave, enterprising, and determined to acquire the top female (the Princess) and put her in their own castle forever after. They always, always got the girl in the end. This was because they never stopped until they had accomplished the three stipulated tasks.

Modern-day Alpha Males respond to this format. They actually *want* to be faced with insurmountable odds in order to win the female of their choice. If you make it too easy for them, they feel, at some unacknowledged level, cheated of their Alpha Male right to overcome the impossible.

And here is the reason this means so much to them: Alpha Males *need to know that they are better than other males*. It isn't enough that they actually *are* superior in most ways – in terms of intelligence, strength, ability to capitalize on change effectively and quickly, leadership, and so on — they need to prove it irrefutably to all the world.

So, when he does propose…

So, when your Alpha Male shows signs of wanting to marry you, place a few obstacles in his way. Make him overcome some minor challenges.

First of all, make him propose, literally, on one knee, a symbolic gesture of his recognition that you stand on a pedestal and are his equal, and are therefore worthy of his great efforts to win you. Then come up with three challenges he has to meet and overcome. He's only going to propose once; make it memorable and symbolic. Make it clear it is a very important moment for you both.

Challenges that involve a feat of strength or endurance are best because these are areas where most Alpha Males excel. Make him slay a figurative dragon or demolish a figurative foe. If he works out at a gym, tell him he has to achieve a record of pushups or bench-presses that is higher than he currently can claim.

When you do have your wedding, remember to keep your Alpha Male as your primary focus. Don't make the mistake many women do — that of getting so caught up in the details of planning the event that they sideline their husband-to-be. It would be better to run away and get married than to ignore him in the months leading up to the wedding.

The pre-nuptial agreement.

What about a _pre-nuptial agreement_ (sometimes called a _pre-nup?_) Should you agree to one if your husband-to-be wants it? Should you yourself decide to initiate one?

A pre-nuptial agreement addresses in legally binding detail a great many questions relating to property, money, and disposition of assets in a marriage.

It is always a good idea to know the legal ramifications of _anything_ you do before you do it. Marriage is such a deeply important, life-changing decision that it makes sense to consult an attorney specializing in marital law even if all you do is ask questions about marriage law in your state (laws vary from state to state, believe it or not). At a minimum, you will gain interesting and useful knowledge.

If you already own considerable assets, or if either of you has children from a previous marriage, a pre-nuptial agreement may be needed or advisable to spell out in advance the rights of the children. His children may see you as a threat to their inheritance; this is one reason to consider a pre-nuptial agreement.

But if your husband-to-be asks you to sign anything, be sure that you do consult an attorney (your own attorney, hired independently by you, not one you both share) before you sign. If you are being asked to sign away fair rights as half of the married team, it is unfair to you.

Don't sign anything that does not do justice to you and to any children you may have in the future together. If your future husband does not intend to treat you with full respect as a wife and equal partner, your marriage will be unequal from the start, and you may come to regret having agreed to an unfair pre-nuptial agreement at all.

6.

TRAINING
YOUR ALPHA MALE

There is a woman in New York City who was one of NBC's top television producers of all time. She obtained many 'firsts' for the network, filming documentaries in Iron Curtain countries before anyone else and delivering exciting programming with some of the most important stars of the day, time after time, in television specials. She was tall, with flaming red hair and an impressive figure. She looked as if she could have been an opera diva, had she gone into another line of work.

Her personality matched her other attributes — when things got too dull around her office, she would get on the phone to someone in a position of power on the West Coast and start a yelling match. Once she actually pulled the phone out of the wall and threw it across the room, hitting the other wall. She enjoyed this kind of excitement; she did it for the fun of it, between projects. Occasionally her friends would drop by just to say hello: Mary Tyler Moore, Bette Davis, Shirley MacLaine, Norah Ephron, Mikhail Baryshnikov. If ever there was an Alpha Female, it was she.

She was married to a man originally from Russia, a potent patron of the arts and powerful friend to many of Russia's most famous ballet dancers. When you met him, you were not aware of his physical stature; he struck you immediately as a big man, although he stood just over five feet tall. His personality was genuinely charming, and as quiet as his wife's was flamboyant. Without shadow of a doubt, he was an Alpha Male.

One day when his wife was busy browbeating a film director in Los Angeles on the phone, he called on another line. The secretary handed her a note saying her husband was on the line. "Goodbye, Howard," she said abruptly into the telephone, and hung up. She punched in another line, and could be heard through the open office door saying in soft, cooing tones, "Hello, my <u>darling</u>, what a nice surprise to hear from you! I was just <u>wishing</u> I could hear the sound of your voice when you called..."

Their long marriage contained great fun and excitement and happiness. And it proves that an Alpha Male and an equally strong Alpha Female can find a truly happy life together. While their particular pattern would be hard for others to replicate, for them it was ideal.

* * *

<u>Now that you have married your Alpha Male, how do you make your day-to-day life work?</u>

How do you keep your identity strong and intact if your Alpha Male tries to boss you around? How do you deal with unfair criticism from your Alpha Male? It is time to begin training your Alpha Male in earnest.

A well-trained Alpha Male is the world's best husband. Here are proven strategies for dealing with the Alpha Male's natural dominance — and techniques for establishing trust through loyalty. You'll see how humor plays an important role in a successful marriage.

<u>Guidelines for a happy life with your Alpha Male.</u>

You've seen couples who have a magic about them — who seem to be perpetually in love, yet remain confident and self-assured as individuals. Usually the woman in these couples is very savvy about what steps are necessary to make a marriage work. The following guidelines show how to keep your Alpha Male happy without compromising yourself.

- *Make him happy.* Be the star and joy of his life. Make him glad every day that he married you. Let him know on a daily basis that no other male measures up to him in your eyes. This is an on-going need of all Alpha Males — to be on top, to be the best — and he needs to hear it from you every day in some form.

- *Respect his work.* An Alpha Male's income is the engine that supports both of you. Respect that, and give him the accolades that he deserves. Celebrate his achievements. If he tells you of some success he has had at work, drop everything and really listen. Alpha Males don't often tell you much; if he does, it means it really matters to him. Give him your full attention and lots of praise. Ask a few questions.

> *A woman married to one Alpha Male and mother of two more says:*
>
> *"Allow him to know that he's Alpha in his household. Let him be the CEO of the dinner table. Allow him his idiosyncrasies. Find those idiosyncrasies charming rather than giving him a hard time about them."*

- *Praise him.* Give your Alpha Male honest compliments, at least one or two a day. Recognize his best qualities. Some examples: "That's a brilliant idea. You really are *so* smart." "I love your looks." "You sure are a sexy guy." "I love the way you walk." "I'm so lucky to have met you." "Men

admire you. I can tell by the respect they show."
"Absolutely *no one* would mess with you."

- *Be amusing.* When you talk, make it interesting. Entertain him. Don't go on about the day's problems. Tell him a new fact daily (he'll look forward to finding out something from you on a regular basis — check encyclopedias and newspapers if you need ideas). Make your conversation a way of connecting with your Alpha Male, full of facts and observations that make his day more interesting. Topics to stay away from: gossip about people you know, your health problems (unless there is a significant reason he must know), "innermost feelings," and above all, 'the relationship' — a colossal bore to Alpha Males.

A well-known author, long before his work made him famous, spotted a young woman across the room at a party. She had the most beautiful smile and dancing eyes he had ever seen. He crossed the room, took her hand in his, and poured a handful of peanuts into her palm. "I wish they were emeralds," he told her.

In time they married. After many years of their long and happy life together, he crossed the room, took her hand in his, and poured a handful of emeralds into her palm.

" I wish they were peanuts," he said.

- *Be interesting.* Keep developing your own interests by doing new things or continuing to learn more about your present interests. Try learning something entirely new (and don't tell him until after you've been doing it awhile — he will be amazed, and will wonder what *else* you might be doing of which he is unaware — this is part of keeping your mystique with him). Some ideas: Study Chinese; breed Siamese fighting fish, learn Feng Shui, take a fly-fishing course and learn to tie flies, take up boxing, take a course in mechanics or car repair. Learn about something he doesn't think you can, like motorcycle maintenance (with or without Zen), or learn scrabble or dog training or chess. Enter a competition and try to win it. Alpha Males approve of winning, and of people who keep on trying to win right down to the wire, even if they don't succeed in the end. Making a full-out effort catches the full attention of an Alpha Male. If you *do* win something, whatever it is, don't be surprised to hear your Alpha Male saying in a proud, offhand manner to another male, "*Oh, my wife just won the ....*"

- *Have outside friends.* Do exciting things elsewhere with other people; let it drop afterward that you've just done something ultra-cool and interesting (don't mention it beforehand, though).

- *Give him space.* Spend part of your time in different parts of the house or apartment. Let him just vegetate sometimes in front of the television or with a book. Leave him space to be alone and not think or react. Don't bug him when he's 'distant' by asking him what's the matter. Just make him comfortable and leave him alone. Tell him where to find you and leave.

> *Ipse Dixit*
> **ALPHA MALES IN THEIR OWN WORDS**
>
> *"Give him respite. He's been snarling and biting at other males all day, and he'd like to come home to some peace and a rest."*

- *Keep sex interesting.* Once in a while, after you're married, surprise him in sex. It's okay to be inventively silly. Here are a handful of actual cases that were big hits: One woman wrapped herself in Saran Wrap with a big red bow and met her husband at the door. Another dressed up as a French parlor maid in nothing but a frilly apron, lace cap, and high-heeled shoes, bearing an ostrich duster on a stick. One wife turned the bedroom into a bordello with red lights, pillows everywhere, incense, and honky-tonk music. Another woman took her husband on a picnic to remote fields of hay and slowly stripped him in the tall grass. Don't ever let your husband think he has learned all there is to know about you. Keep him slightly off balance with enjoyable surprises.

> *The wife of a well-known tycoon, famous for his ferocity in business, was overheard telling her husband of forty years, "You know, you really are the sweetest man in the whole world—and I'm the only one who knows it!"*

- *Care for your Alpha Male.* Keep your Alpha Male well fed and well exercised. Get him to work out, walk, run, swim, play basketball with his friends. See to it he takes vitamins with trace minerals. Make him eat organic food if possible. He's too busy paying attention to the jungle he works in to focus on much else. You can do a lot to keep him healthy and fit, and if you don't take charge of it, it may not happen at all. Don't let him get out of shape.

- *Be a good sport.* Be generous about the things he likes to do and wants you to do with him, even if you *hate* watching that stupid television show or going to the computer store. Go along with his plans with good grace; if you are surly or complain, it negates the good effect of your company.

- *Plan outings.* Take him places by making all the arrangements so all he has to do is show up. Make trips a treat for him, where he can be entertained and relax after the strenuous rat-race of his daily work.

- *Offer encouragement when he fails.* Never tell an Alpha Male that his failures don't matter. Because his failures *do* matter. Say, "*Next time you will succeed. You know you will.*"

> *A marriage license doesn't give you ownership; it gives you privilege.*
>
> —*Alpha wife of one of nation's leading (Alpha Male) surgeons*

- *Give him time to be with his male buddies.* Pack him off with a smile if he wants to take a guys' trip camping, fishing, or mountain climbing.

- *Welcome him.* Greet him every time he appears with a genuine smile or a hug, even if he's just been out getting gas for the car. Like Alpha wolves, who are met by the entire pack whenever they return from a hunting trip, your Alpha Male will bask in this form of attention.

- *Be a good hostess.* Entertain his business associates if it will help his work. This is much easier to do successfully than most people realize. All it takes is good food and making sure your guests feel important, clever, and well-liked.

- *Be honest.* Give honest criticism (see Chapter Five). Always be honest but tactful. Correct an incorrect action; don't belittle or treat your Alpha Male with contempt.

- *Stand up for yourself.* Don't accept from him any form of putdown or belittling of yourself. Call him on it immediately (see Chapter Eight for details).

Establishing and maintaining trust with your Alpha Male.

Establishing trust takes a long time. It can be broken in an instant. Guard the trust you have built with your Alpha Male. It is your most valuable possession. Do nothing to put it into jeopardy. Once broken, trust can be patched up but never made whole again. Resentments may be buried, but they will remain under the surface and can show up in twisted ways later on.

So be very careful not to divulge personal information about your Alpha Male to anyone outside the family. That would violate your Alpha Male's sense of trust. To tell his secrets is to make him vulnerable, and will be seen as betrayal.

(The one obvious exception to this is when by mutual agreement you have consulted an outside person — a counselor, family member, or friend — for the express purpose of having an outside opinion on some problem you both agree needs solving and cannot be solved without help).

Absolute loyalty is the biggest component of trust. Without loyalty, there is no trust. Here's why: At the bottom of this need is the fact that any female an Alpha Male chooses and desires is bound to be the best female. Therefore all other males will also notice her. Any of them can circle the camp, find an opportunity to strike, and bingo! he, the Alpha Male may, unbeknownst to himself, be raising some other male's children. This is not a conscious thought. Even if it were, no Alpha Male would ever admit this fear. But this fear is absolutely fundamental to him.

> *Among the Pacific Northwest's Native Americans in the 1700's and 1800's a sort of Alpha Male competition took place called a <u>potlatch</u>. Valuable property—blankets, hides, copper goods—were displayed, and then destroyed by the owners; whoever was willing to destroy more of his own wealth, in a putdown of their neighboring communities, was the winner. (The practice was finally made illegal).*

<u>Getting your Alpha Male to help with chores.</u>

A man will never offer another man help unless it is specifically asked for. To do so would insult the man who was put in the position of being assisted by implying that he was weak and in need of help. Therefore, unless he has been specifically trained on this point, your Alpha Male may not offer to help you unless you actually ask him point blank. So *don't* say to him, "Can't you *see* I need help pulling this huge trash can up the driveway?" Instead, say, "Hey, give me a hand with this, will you? It's hard for me to move it." (That is, tell him exactly what you want him to do rather than imply he is dense for not figuring it out for himself. It isn't that he doesn't notice; he just thinks you prefer to handle things for yourself unless you actually ask his help.).

By the same token, don't offer to help an Alpha Male unless he actually, specifically asks for your help. Just say, "I'm here if you need me, let me know." In the same way, never offer advice on his job, unless he asks for it. Just make a calm, nourishing (to both body and soul) atmosphere at home so he can solve his work problems, until he asks for your opinion and advice.

> *How does a woman make an Alpha Male happy? She makes his life interesting. She handles every aspect of his life and makes it all, including the sexual one, interesting.*
> *—Wife of an Alpha Male (and mother of two others)*

Lighten up! Have a good laugh instead of getting angry.

You can handle sticky situations with humor and a sense of fun instead of anger, if you decide to. Here's an example from an Alpha Male (one of the leading surgeons in the country, he operated on presidents and the heads of state all over the world) and his Alpha wife (head of the operating room at a major hospital).

She tells the story: "I saw one of the nurses was flirting with my husband. So I told my husband, '*I saw* her coming on to you. You'd better be careful, or I'm going to *kill* you.'

"So he said, 'That's why I'm wearing this *armor* underneath my clothes.' "

It's a lot more fun to be around someone who turns a potential argument into a good laugh instead. In another instance, the Alpha wife of an Alpha husband needed to take their enormous dog (a harlequin Great Dane) out for a walk, but she knew her husband would be looking for her as soon as he returned home to do some accounting work he needed for a deadline. She left him a note: On a small sheet of paper, she drew a grid showing the five or six streets she planned to walk with the dog. Across the top she wrote in block letters: "Harley and I are walking somewhere on this grid. Come and find us and cover us with kisses." (When he found her, it was with a smile.)

<u>How to handle unfair criticism.</u>

Alpha Males sometimes criticize, and sometimes the criticism is unfair. This can hurt. Here is how to handle it:

If he launches into you with a personal attack or says something critical that is just plain untrue, say to him calmly, "Tell me what is on your mind."

Do not react with hostility and do not, above all, show him that he has hurt you.

When he starts his critique, begin to *write down* what he accuses you of; make no verbal comment, except to say, when he finally pauses, "Can you be more specific?" which will send him off on another long tirade. Your purpose is to get absolutely all the venom out of him, however misdirected it is. If he repeats himself, ignore it. Stay calm. Keep writing it all down.

When he finally can't think of any more insults, tell him, "I will give careful thought to what you've just said. I will get back to you." (Do *not* say "...to your unfair accusations" or "to your ridiculous criticisms" — keep your language and tone completely neutral.)

There are four reasons for handling unfair or hurtful criticism in this way:

First: It avoids a noisy row, which he will win because he can yell louder. (If it is *you* who likes the noisy rows, get a new hobby. This one can destroy a marriage. Yes, there is a moment of euphoria after a fight, but the hurtful things said are never completely forgotten.)

Second: You will prevent him from knowing what he said that really hurt you or made you furious (so he won't be able to push your buttons on these subjects if he's tempted to in the future).

Third: It gives you time to weigh the validity of his criticism and to refute illogical accusations calmly, or to respond reasonably to valid criticisms, even if he made them in the wrong way.

Fourth: You do not reward him for picking on you. It's no fun for the attacker if the person he attacks doesn't get upset or visibly angry. *This is the first step in training your Alpha Male to discuss issues instead of fighting* — more about this in Chapter Eight.

The Alpha Male as father

Among the strongest characteristics of every Alpha Male is the desire to build a strong, sound pack and protect and provide for it. Because Alpha Males are themselves at the top of the hierarchy — stronger, smarter, more able, more dominant than other males — they assume it is their right to have the most desirable female — the best looking, most fertile, healthiest — as their mate.

When Alpha Males have children, they assume, in the same way, that they will have the best children, and that they will be raised in their own image. This does not mean, however, that most Alpha Male fathers take an immediate interest in the care and feeding of infants, even their own. (It should be noted that Alpha Males are almost never interested in raising the children of other males as their own; many have trouble accepting fully the children of a woman who has children from a former marriage, for instance. Although there are exceptions to this, they are rare).

Some Alpha Male fathers find the whole business of infants — drooling, squalling, messing their diapers — truly objectionable, and will do anything possible to avoid taking an active part in their day-to-day care. It is therefore an unwise plan to expect an Alpha Male husband to 'do his share' by changing every other diaper. Let your Alpha Male do his fair share in some other way, unless of course he is one of the exceedingly rare examples of the breed who actively enjoys infant care (there are some).

When an Alpha Male's children grow big enough to begin to engage in more interesting activities like crawling, walking, speaking, and so forth, the Alpha Male father begins to take an active interest. Here is something he knows about — speed, endurance, and athletic ability (even if the speed is in crawling across the floor, the endurance is in valiant attempts to stand up, and the athletic ability is in actually managing to do it).

When his children are big enough to throw a baseball, pass a football, kick a soccer ball, ride a pony, row a dinghy, or paddle a canoe, the Alpha Male father begins to shine as a parent. Here he is on his own turf. He takes a deep interest in his children as they develop physical skills. He himself excels at these things as a rule, and he enjoys teaching his offspring how to do the things he likes. The list may extend to reading, writing poetry, learning to play a musical instrument, skiing, diving, building a fire, climbing a tree, swimming, and any number of other actions requiring speed, strength, endurance, athletic ability, and intelligence.

Many Alpha Males are excellent fathers, enjoying their kids' achievements and encouraging them to develop their skills. The ideal combination of demonstration, encouragement, technical pointers, and practice can be a strong bonding experience between an Alpha Male father and his children. When you see a middle-aged woman who throws a baseball like a pro, it's often a fair assumption she is the daughter of an Alpha Male.

If your Alpha Male becomes too focused on winning, however, you may need to train him to remember that his son or daughter is still a kid, and that too much early pressure will have the opposite effect from what he intends. Kids who are made to feel overwhelmed by pressure to win sometimes withdraw or grow to hate the game (in the worst cases, they can even grow to dislike their father if he endlessly criticizes and browbeats). Is there ever a time to tell a child he didn't do what he should have? Yes, but the ratio of praise to criticism should be overwhelmingly weighted on the side of praise.

Encouragement and appreciation work much better; and remember to appreciate and praise your Alpha Male, too, for encouraging the children without making them feel inadequate. If your Alpha Male forgets this important point, remind him as often as needed, in a scheduled meeting (see Chapter Eight).

Some Alpha Male fathers are so consumed by their work that they actually must be trained to schedule enough time to be with their families. Treat this as a business appointment, insofar as the scheduling is concerned. Plan activities he will enjoy with his children (you will have to make all the logistical arrangements; an Alpha Male is working extremely hard almost all the time at his job). Be sure to praise your Alpha Male for making time away to be away from his job to be with his family. Yes, that sounds odd, but it reflects the reality of any Alpha Male's life: he spends virtually all his waking hours 'being' his job. He cannot be separated from his work. To break away from this mindset, even for something as obviously necessary and advisable as being with his children, requires an active effort for an Alpha Male. Time is the hardest thing for an Alpha Male to find.

Some Alpha Male fathers have real difficulty when they see their daughter fall in love with a young man and decide to marry him. It goes against his Alpha Male grain — his daughter is part of *his* pack, after all, and who *is* this young interloper circling the camp and making off with one of his women, anyhow? You will, however, be happy to see how an Alpha Male investigates thoroughly the young man's ability to support your daughter, because this is very important to him. You may find yourself having to stroke some raised fur, and calm your Alpha Male's innate instinct to drive off the invading male. If the fiance and your Alpha Male husband share some interests, it helps make the transition easier for him. Don't expect him to like it, though, at least until he gets used to the idea, sees how happy your daughter is, and gets to know his son-in-law. A son's marriage usually upsets an Alpha Male father less — if he likes the young woman.

<u>A story of an Alpha Male and his son.</u>

An Alpha Male father, working two jobs, came home to perform yet a third job (this had been going on all week): He was laying down a tile floor in two rooms of his house. After dinner, he began work. The tiles were hard and breakable, but with careful heating over a small open flame could be made temporarily soft enough to be cut to fit around radiators and pipes. The tiles were held down with a smelly black glue that on this particular evening he was laying down with a trowel and painstakingly smoothing out so the tiles would adhere evenly. It was a laborious, time-consuming job.

The next morning he came down to find that his three-year-old son was sitting on the newly laid floor, a wooden spool (for thread) in one hand, a butter knife in the other. By laying the knife across the spool, he had been able to gain enough leverage to pry up nearly half of the tiles.

The child's mother came down and saw the destruction. She found her Alpha Male husband in the kitchen, peacefully reading the newspaper and drinking coffee. "What in the world happened?" she asked, horrified. Did Jamie do that?" He nodded.

"What did you do?" she asked.

"Why, I sat down and helped him," said her husband. "How could you not help someone who had just discovered the principle of the fulcrum?"

An Alpha Male (seagull) gets the cake

At the seashore, a woman had a party cake left over that she didn't want to take home after the weekend. She dumped it from the second-story deck onto the driveway below for the birds to eat. Within seconds, a large flock of laughing gulls (Larus atricilla) had descended on the cake. The Alpha gull, a large male, flew at every other gull who attempted to reach the cake, defending it with his sharp beak, making ferocious dives at the other gulls' eyes. For a solid hour he lunged at bird after bird; when one was driven off, another had taken his place.

Finally all the other birds had decided they'd better keep their distance from the tantalizing meal. The Alpha gull dove at the food, gobbled huge chunks of cake and frosting, all the while looking menacingly in this direction or that at a would-be cake attack. When he couldn't eat any more, he took off toward the beach.

Immediately he was replaced by another gull who attempted to do the same thing. His movements were less sure, and occasionally another gull would manage to grab a beak-full while the number-two gull was busy chasing off somebody else. Finally he, too, ate his fill and flew off.

Instantly number-three gull took center stage. He was far less skilled than the first two, and many gulls managed to sneak chunks of cake while he was occupied with chasing off other gulls. This continued until almost the last gull, by which time it looked more like a free-for-all than a disciplined defense.

The Alpha Male gull had undoubtedly had the best part of the cake. But he had to work awfully hard to do it.

Your Alpha Male also works awfully hard to stay on top. He is always on duty, except for those brief times when he is home with you and you make him feel he can let his guard down. Make him feel cherished for his unceasing work to provide for and protect you and your home together.

7.

101 TRAINING TIPS FOR YOUR ALPHA MALE

A Checklist to Make Life With an Alpha Male Fun and Productive.

Do

Do realize that, as familiar as the items on this list may be, these concepts have been around for a long time for good reason: They generally work.

Do try to influence your husband. Studies have shown that the only happy, stable marriages are those in which the husband accepts influence from his wife. Just do it in the right way.

Do use the two-year period while romantic love is strongest – his mind attracted by how you look, move, or talk, which triggers an overwhelming hormonal and intense physical interest – to find out everything about him, what he thinks and believes is important, and how he would behave in different situations. After this, the magnetic attraction begins to dissipate on both sides. Build strong connections early.

Do, relative to the above point, be sure that you *like* the Alpha Male you have chosen, quite apart from any biological attraction you have for him. Is he courageous, a good provider, willing to listen (under specific circumstances of discussion as explained in Chapter Eight), loyal, kind, a good friend to share time with? These will matter a great deal over the long haul. Don't marry a man you don't like as well as love.

Do coddle him – that is, do small kind things for him when you know he wants them. It can be as small as saying a cheerful word, or as large as going out of your way to do something with him you'd never do yourself by choice.

Do fix his favorite foods. (Serve even those that are bad for him, in small quantities. If he loves French fries, give him a big salad first and just three or four perfect fries afterward.)

Do create a place that is just his, even if it is just a special chair and reading lamp.

Do try expressing yourself more physically and less verbally with him.

Do respond warmly if he initiates sex – *after marriage but not before.*

Do tell him every single day something you admire about him. (It's okay to repeat.)

Do be a good sport — go with him on outings he enjoys, even if you aren't especially fond of them (sailing, football games, golf, skiing, hiking, etc).

Do notice anything he does well and mention it in words afterwards.

Do speak approvingly of his ability to best his opponents.

Do keep quiet when he's tired.

Do choose your battles (or better still, avoid all battles, and simply choose your subjects for discussion).

Do hire or persuade someone other than him to help with menial chores around the house or yard if possible, unless he likes to do them.

Do, in cases where there is a truly important disagreement, say, *just once*, exactly what you think.

Do let the small stuff – little annoyances – go unmentioned whenever you can.

Do use humor to make your big annoyances known.

Do put yourself on a pedestal and stay there. This means, be the same desirable, slightly elusive, fascinating, and attractive person he married for each and every day of your married life. Yes, realities of life can make it harder at times. No, you don't have to become a lesser person than he married. Be above pettiness, cattiness, selfishness, and banality.

Do laugh at his jokes. Even if he's not a great joke teller, find the bit that's genuinely funny and applaud that.

Do keep his interests in mind when making plans.

Do give him massages (or get a professional to if you can afford it).

Do keep a part of yourself elusive after marriage (don't tell all the daily boring details of your day).

Do something interesting on your own without telling him (join an organization, learn a language or a new skill, do a creative project with photography or house construction or computers, etc.) – and only let it leak out later that you've been doing this for some time. This makes him wonder what *else* he doesn't know about you. This makes you continually fascinating, never completely knowable to him. It encourages a bit of mystique to hover about you.

Do entertain him when you talk to him, as much after marriage as before. If you find this hard to do, think how what you say would look if written down — interesting? enlightening? funny? Or banal? tedious? boring? repetitious?

Do encourage him if he himself decides to cook, take a rake to the leaves, or cut the grass.

Do tell him that you appreciate whatever he does well; show that you noticed and approve of it.

Do give him a break if possible by letting a discussion of a topic on which you differ wait for a while. Say, "We don't have to talk about this right now. Let's go get some ice cream instead." This will make his response to the discussion later on much easier.

Do consider getting a job (if you don't already have a career or job), even part time to cover personal expenses.

Do keep him as number one priority if you have a full-time job with heavy responsibility – this can be a simple as taking the time to explain to him that you're on a deadline and will 'resurface' soon.

Do make sure to take some time with him but apart from everyone else to recharge your own collective sense of yourselves.

Do take him out on a date where you pay everything and make no demands on him whatsoever, but only compliment and nurture him. Be sure to do this from time to time especially *after* you are married.

Do be one hundred percent loyal to your Alpha Male.

Do demand one hundred percent loyalty from him.

Do make your case for things you need, by discussion, not argument.

Do spend some time apart from him either alone or with your own friends.

Do go for walks daily if you're both able to physically. Lots of men think more openly when on their feet and moving forward. (Physical fitness benefits everyone in any case. And exercise is one of the best stress-relievers there is.) Fifteen minutes before breakfast is a good start.

Do remember, male brains even before birth are different from female brains. Males cannot do many things women take for granted, like distinguishing nuances of facial expressions or tone variations of voice. Where you thought that your 'pointed look' should have told him you were upset about something he said, it simply doesn't register with your Alpha Male.

Do remember that Alpha Males are generally stronger and more single-minded than anyone else once their course is set. If, despite all attempts to discuss and resolve a disagreement, the process fails, get outside professional help (a counselor who specializes in problem-solving, for example) who can act as a referee.

Do get prior agreement with your Alpha Male before seeing an outside counselor. And both go to see the counselor together, at least initially.

Do use as little correction as possible when training your Alpha Male, and stop as soon as you can see the new thought you are teaching him is entering his head.

Do stop while you are ahead during a discussion — do not try to get outright agreement; let the subject rest.

Do treat an Alpha Male boss in the workplace with respect. He is trying to lead his pack of employees and achieve some goal he is pursuing. The more your actions show you are in line with his aims, the less friction.

Do know that if you challenge an Alpha Male boss, he will treat you as he would another attacking Alpha Male. It is all about position in the pack: There is only room for one pack leader. He will want to symbolically kill you off. Challenge if you like, but be prepared for a battle to the death (like getting fired).

Do remember: Alpha Males must pursue. The equation will not work unless you create conditions for this to happen. Marriages that take place when he did not pursue feel like entrapment to an Alpha Male.

Do pay attention once you are married to the Alpha Male of your choice. Sliding into complacency is a kind of selfishness. An Alpha Male is the top-of-the-line choice. Make sure to appreciate yours.

Do give him time to be with his friends.

Do make it clear that you expect him to succeed and not to fail. Success is important to him. He expects it of himself. If he fails, he needs to hear encouragement that he will succeed next time, that you are on his side, that you are there for him if he needs you, that you have ideas to help him if he wants them (let him ask; Alpha Males don't like having ideas shoved at them).

Don't

Don't fall in love with your chosen Alpha Male first; make him fall in love with you first. (*Then* fall in love with him.)

Don't belittle him verbally, not once, not ever.

Don't make him look bad in front of anyone (including the kids).

Don't attempt to hold a discussion if either of you has had alcohol recently.

Don't allow him to intimidate you or make you subservient; he won't respect you.

Don't, while dating, talk about your own past or about yourself. Keep the spotlight for quite a while squarely on his early life, experiences, interests, and values.

Don't place your children above him. He needs to be respected as what he is: leader of his pack.

Don't discuss the "state of your relationship." Alpha Males deeply dislike and are bored by this kind of discussion, and it threatens their feeling of security within their pack.

Don't discuss your innermost feelings with an Alpha Male, for the same reason.

Don't expect him to listen patiently to your worries.

Don't expect him to do housework. If you can get him to do *some*, you're ahead of the curve.

Don't have sex with him before marriage if you intend to marry him. He will think at some level that other males could also have 'got' you without marriage if he could. This will make him think less of *himself.* Yes, many women go against this rule, and sometimes it works out anyway. Many times it does not. An Alpha Male actually *likes* to idealize his wife. The 'No sex until married' rule helps him to do this.

Don't tell a funnier joke just after he has told one, even if he mangled it. Just laugh at his joke.

Don't compare him to his friends. That is, don't say "Joe is so much better at the computer/a driver/a card player) than you are."

Don't keep him waiting When you say you'll be ready, be ready.

Don't break your promises.

Don't try to argue with him head-on.

Don't interrupt if he is trying, even clumsily, to verbalize something he can't easily say. Just listen, nod your head to show you understand what he is driving at, but let him say it his own way.

Don't initiate a discussion about anything important on the run. Get his attention, set a specific time frame (keep it short), and take a walk together side by side while you talk.

Don't patronize him. That is, don't act as though you think he is stupid. He isn't. As one Alpha Male put it, "He's just emotionally retarded." In fact, he isn't retarded, he is just as emotionally developed as any other Alpha Male. He is better at other things than you are. And he does operate in a very different way from you.

Don't tell him everything on your mind all the time; choose interesting or entertaining things to talk about and be quiet when you don't need to say anything.

Don't speak your mind until you can do it quietly and when you have his full attention.

Don't whine.

Don't complain. Call a scheduled meeting and discuss what you need or want.

Don't finish his sentences for him.

Don't say: "Let me finish." If he is yelling as you try to make your point in a disagreement, simply repeat what you are saying in a normal voice until you sense it is sinking in. Then stop.

Don't try to discuss anything for more than six or seven minutes at a time. Make your points within this time.

Don't expect or ask for agreement when you have made your points in a disagreement. He needs time to think it over. To push will earn you a negative reply.

Don't try to get to the bottom of things on topics that involve the emotions. Your Alpha Male will tune out.

Don't tell personal and private information about him to outsiders; he will feel betrayed.

Don't expect him to think or act as you do. He is a very, very different critter.

Don't lecture him.

Don't use tears or anguish to motivate (manipulate) him.

Don't be surprised if he yells at you. Calmly explain in a scheduled meeting that you don't like it, don't function well when he does it, and if he wants to motivate you to do or not do something, he should tell you in words and *not* yell.

Don't cut him off if he is trying to tell you something. Remain silent so he can think; many men have trouble verbalizing.

Don't pick up his dirty laundry after he has stepped out of it. Either do something creative with it (hang it on a small Christmas tree in the middle of the room, for instance — or create a giant centipede out of all the shoes he has stepped out of and left behind). Make your point in a meeting within a scheduled time frame.

Don't be surprised if the point above doesn't work. He is marking his territory, and this is an inborn trait in Alpha Males.

Don't mention every little thing he does that irritates you. Ignore what you can that isn't important.

Don't be the middleman between your husband and children or parents-in-law. Let them deal directly with each other as much as possible.

Don't ever forget that Alpha Males excel at confrontation. So don't play this game. Use logic, timing, and an occasional compliment to win disagreements.

Don't yell at an Alpha Male, for the above reason. He can yell louder, and has more muscles to flex.

Don't give up on trying to modify his behavior if it is truly important (differences on child rearing, for example). Just call formal meetings with a set time frame and try again.

Don't think an Alpha Male has lost or lacks his chief characteristics either when he is very old or when he is very young. Alpha Males are born the way they are. Surrounding circumstances (health, age, strength, etc.) change, but the Alpha Male's basic drives do not.

Don't let him know everything you are thinking. Be a bit elusive from time to time.

Don't notice him first (even if you have and are secretly smitten – keep it secret). Let him notice you first (use the means outlined in Chapter Three). Then give him time to plan and begin his pursuit of you.

Don't chase after an Alpha Male. He won't value you if you do.

Don't disregard the warning signs of a relationship not going well.

Don't wait to take the actions outlined in Chapter Five if things are not progressing well.

Don't be afraid to walk away early on. Unless he is pursuing you the relationship will not work.

Don't 'close the door' when you walk away from your Alpha Male – leave it open enough so he can come back after he's had time to realize how much he misses you and wants you in his life. Do this even if it takes him a long time, if you intend to marry him.

Don't hang on and keep trying if you can see that he will not pursue you no matter what you do. If an Alpha Male doesn't cherish you, you will be at a bad disadvantage throughout your marriage. Pain of parting is far better than a lonely marriage. But leave the door open a crack, just in case. Alpha Males are notoriously slow to learn some things.

Don't be afraid to move on, using the techniques in this book. Look diligently for a new Alpha Male who captures your interest, imagination, and heart (believe it or not, there is more than one 'perfect' match for each of us in the world). The trick is to find him. This book will help you to do it.

8.

HAPPINESS WITH AN ALPHA MALE

Can you actually win an argument with an Alpha Male? This chapter shows you step by step how to do it. You *can* win at least some of the time, but not by confronting him head on. You'll learn how Alpha Males regard the concept of *talking* in a way that is completely different from women's understanding of the word. This chapter is packed with practical tactics for staking out your own turf in the relationship, while keeping your Alpha Male happy and unthreatened.

The late great dog trainer Vicki Hearne said in one of her books that the trainer must *correct the dog's error in behavior*, but *never punish the dog*. The distinction is important: If you correct an action, you are telling the miscreant "You have done something you must not do. That action must stop. Instead of that action, do this acceptable action instead."

Compare the above with punishment. Punishment, by contrast, tells the offender: "You are bad, stupid, incorrigible, and worthless, and I don't like you because of it." Punishment, said Hearne, "spreads a deep gloom." And it does not work as a training tool.

The Alpha Male (human) you are training reacts in exactly the same way that his canine associates do. If punished, he will growl, get thoroughly disgusted, and pee on everything (in many cases, symbolically), or become deeply unhappy.

> *Always use as little correction as possible. Start by making one point, not all your points at once. Keep your ammunition dry. Only use a second point if necessary to tip the scale ever-so-slightly in favor of your argument. Learn to recognize the moment that the point you are making actually enters the brain of the Alpha Male – generally you can sense a momentary pause in the counteroffensive barrage – and quit while you are ahead.*

How to keep your Alpha Male happy while correcting him.

Apart from the humane consideration that it is kinder to make your Alpha Male happy than unhappy, it is nearly impossible to live with an unhappy Alpha Male. Therefore it is in your own interest to learn the tricks of the trade for keeping an Alpha Male happy. If he is happy he will want to be with his pack – you, plus juveniles of both sexes – and be less inclined to go off looking for fun and excitement elsewhere. You will strengthen his natural instinctive drive to build and protect his pack. There is no one as much fun and exciting to be with as an Alpha Male who feels all is right with his world.

But you must not ever become a doormat, humbly taking on all the chores and saying, "Yes, master" when he doesn't do his fair share of them. It matters very much how you go about this, however. Do it right and he will do his share, although it may be in a different form from yours. Handle it wrong, and he will become obstinate, angry, or withdraw.

Let's say you have talked briefly about some subject, perhaps as simple as where to go for the weekend, or as complicated as whether to move across country for a better job for one of you.

Or let's say you are engaged to marry, and out of the blue your Alpha Male tells you he expects you to sign a prenuptial agreement that you disagree with on principle. You suspect that if you raise the subject again, you'll be met with resistance or outright refusal, or even an attempt to intimidate you by bellowing at you.

Can you win a disagreement under the circumstances? Yes, you can. But it won't be by confronting your Alpha Male. Alpha Males are experts in confrontation, don't forget. Don't go onto his turf. Bring him onto yours.

> *Ipse Dixit*
> **ALPHA MALES IN THEIR OWN WORDS**
>
> *"Men count on the idea that they are stronger, better, more aggressive. Or that's what they think. Women are, in fact, incredibly aggressive. Think of the mother bear and her cubs."*

<u>So, how do you go about it?</u>

First, stay calm. *You will get nowhere confronting an Alpha Male head-on.* The more you yell, the more he will entrench his position. You can never win an *argument* because categorically you cannot win arguments with an Alpha Male.

> *You cannot win an <u>argument</u> with an Alpha Male. You can only win <u>disagreements</u>. The tools you use are logic, timing, and the occasional compliment.*

You need to go about it differently. You can only win *disagreements*, and this is done with logic, timing, and the occasional compliment. You can in fact succeed in getting your Alpha Male to change his position if you go about it in the right way. You can't win every time, of course, but you can win often enough to keep life interesting.

The physical setup for winning a discussion

To begin with, never have discussions on anything you care about *until you have made clear to your Alpha Male that you want his undivided attention.*

Give him a *time frame*: "I need your undivided attention for seven minutes." If you use an odd-sounding number of minutes, he will be more likely to agree to it. He will be more likely to pay attention (even if at first he is only checking to see whether you do in fact keep within the time you specified). He will think you are very precise and have something precise to say to him. Terms like "ten minutes" are so often bandied about that they carry baggage with them (so he may think, "Oh, no, last time I had to wait ten minutes at the dentist's office it turned out to be an hour and a half.")

Don't ever say "We need to talk about something" because *talking means something very different to the Alpha Male* from what it means to most women. Women talk about things all the time, to learn, to exchange ideas with each other, for solidarity, for support, for comfort. Alpha Males have an entirely different take on talking, however. For an Alpha Male, talking means you become vulnerable: An enemy can hear you making noise and will attack you; you can disclose something you know that the enemy does not; you can make a mistake and have it held against you; you can appear foolish.

Men are by their very brain structure slower to develop verbal skills than women. So an Alpha Male equates talking with danger, and feels vulnerable against an adversary who is "on her own turf." Naturally he doesn't want to talk. He's a man of action. When he is pursuing, he feels confident. When he is talking – especially if the discussion involves some sort of modification of his own actions (Will he be asked to change? Will he want to? Will he find himself without sex if he doesn't?) — he feels out of his element and vulnerable. This uneasiness will make him dig in his heels even more.

> _Talking_ means something very different to an Alpha Male from what it means to you. Talking means being on uncertain ground and playing by rules he instinctively mistrusts. Lawyers may be an exception to this rule, although frequently they are not; they can argue rationally, unemotionally, and brilliantly on almost anything _except_ their own behavior.

Rather than _sitting down_ to talk for your seven (or whatever) minutes, _suggest a walk_. This accomplishes two things that will work in your favor.

> The eyes of animals like a horse or gazelle are set on each side of their head to watch for predators. Those of predators—both dogs and humans—are set on the front of their faces. When a dog prepares to attack another dog, he faces his enemy squarely and makes eye contact.

First, it takes your Alpha Male off his home turf. When he is in his lair, an Alpha Male is more likely to react in his customary ways – getting him off his home turf makes it less likely that his surroundings will trigger entrenched responses, such as turning on the television set.

Second, walking together means you can talk side-by-side rather than face-to-face. Dogs who are about to attack another dog nearly always first face their adversary squarely and make eye contact. It is quite possible that traces of an instinctive reaction to a face-to-face encounter remain in the human Alpha Male.

> *This is an ironclad principle in training Alpha Males: Never make a comment that tears down the Alpha Male's status. The only personal comments you must make are positive ones that show appreciation of his good qualities – strength, loyalty, intelligence, leadership, courage, tenacity. Right in the middle of a discussion on something you disagree about, you can pause momentarily and say, "You know, you really do have amazing biceps."*

When you begin the discussion, describe the situation succinctly and clearly, using as few words as possible. Alpha Males like to cut to the chase; you should forget the unnecessary descriptive words. Use facts and reason. Speak slowly. Use short sentences. This helps let each thought sink in.

For instance, say: "I want to help my parents move their furniture. I know you have planned a beach trip. I hope you'll change your mind and help me out. I'm not as strong physically as you. I'd really appreciate your help. If you will, we can do whatever you want next weekend."

Or

"I really hope you will take that new job. It would mean we could start to save more since it involves a raise. It would be a chance to see a different part of the country. I think I can find a position in my field there. We will not be able to save enough on our present salaries in our present jobs. Will you think about it?"

How to discuss the daily grind and why you must.

Some decisions pertaining to the chores of everyday life may seem too trivial and unimportant to talk about, especially if you think that discussion will be met with resistance. But unless you discuss these issues with your Alpha Male and get agreement on them, you may find yourself doing absolutely all the household chores. Unless you address the fact you want some sort of shared responsibility (assuming you do) it is unfair to expect your Alpha Male to guess what you want. In fact, many maintain that Alpha Males *never* read minds.

As noted earlier, helping with any sort of household work is alien to *all* Alpha Males. You will wait a long time for an Alpha Male either to see the need to help around the house or to see the necessity of doing so.

Women instinctively know that it will not be easy to get agreement on the subject of helping with household chores, and often simply duck the issue for as long as they can.

But these unspoken demands, which is what they really are, cause hidden resentment and often later blow up when the long-suffering chore-doer has finally taken out the garbage one time too many. Household chores by their very nature are repetitious. Therefore they wear a person down slowly.

That there is even a problem will probably go unnoticed by the Alpha Male until the person who has been doing all the chores finally blows up at him. At this point the Alpha Male will ask with genuine bewilderment and some justification, "What in the world has gotten into you? Why are you all of a sudden so angry with (screaming at) me? What did I do?" Alpha Males lack the ability to perceive unstated details; they only pay attention when you spell it out clearly, using as few words as possible and keeping emotion out of it. Say, "Please fix that hole in the floor." Don't say, "Can't you *see* that anyone can break a leg in that hole?" He probably didn't notice much, walked around the hole, and didn't realize you cared about it.

House-training: Feeding the Alpha Male

Alpha Males are actually quite easy to house-train, because when they are done their day's work at the office or doing whatever they do to bring in support for the pack, what they really want most is to be appreciated for being a big strong studly male. They don't actually want to do much except be greeted as the conquering hero, and to be fed and coddled properly.

> *The preferred method of dining at home for young, single Alpha Males is to stand in front of the open refrigerator, consuming a bottle of milk or a loaf of bread, or, in the case of messier items, to dine over the sink so no plates or cutlery are needed and they won't have to mop up the floor afterwards. For more formal occasions, they often wear clothes.*

<u>Consider the subject of cooking dinner every night.</u>

Unless he actually *likes* to cook (and a few Alpha Males excel in this), he wants you to pick up the makings for dinner on the way home from *your* job and put it on the table with a minimum of fuss. He doesn't want to be made to feel he should do more to help, so don't bother him with sighs, 'looks,' or innuendoes. He expects you to clear up afterwards, too. He's busy resting, don't forget, and can't be disturbed while the game is on television. Don't argue with any of this at the time he is ducking out of his fair share of work. Just do it. You'll see why in a minute.

Your Alpha Male should, and will, do his fair share of putting the food on the table if you handle things properly.

One way is to get him to agree to take you to dinner at a local restaurant a certain number of times per week. Another is to bring home already prepared meals. If you have a place to use it, interest him in acquiring an outdoor grill. Get a rice steamer, a hot pot, and any means you can use to make food preparation a low-maintenance affair.

If you really hate and loathe cooking or are terrible at it, it's possible to get a friend who loves to cook to prepare meal-sized plastic bags with his favorite foods, fill the freezer with them, and drop one in boiling water every evening while you make a salad. In each case, the Alpha Male pays the actual expense while you arrange the operation and serve up the food and clear up afterwards.

> *Having a friend prepare meals in plastic bags has some advantages in addition to costing less than store-bought entrees. Meals can be tailored to your Alpha Male's and your own preferences, and can also be more healthful – salt, preservatives, and coloring can be avoided, for example.*

These tactics can offer the Alpha Male a way of buying his way out of actual hands-on service, something like the way soldiers in the Civil War paid someone else to go to war in their place. If the net gain is a fair distribution of work, it makes sense.

Another way to handle inequality of labor in connection with meals: If you really enjoy cooking but dislike other chores, you can negotiate a deal so you handle everything connected with mealtimes, while your Alpha Male takes over getting the car serviced, cutting the grass, getting repairs done on the house, or whatever else needs doing. Decide what chores can be best served by your Alpha Male's strengths – both in the physical

> *Dogs scratch in the dirt after they pee to leave a smell from their paw pads that says, "I'm male. I was here."*
> *Human males do the same thing by leaving the toilet seat up. Do they "forget"? No. It's hardwired behavior. They <u>have</u> to do it ("The testosterone made me do it!")*

sense and in the sense of his enjoying doing them. If your goal is a fair distribution of the workload, it makes sense to end up also, when everything is accomplished, with a happy Alpha Male, not a sulky or resentful one. Everyone wins.

Winning a disagreement with an Alpha Male.

What do you do when your Alpha Male says "*No*" to your reasoned argument in favor of his own point of view? Suppose he says he will not contribute to dinner in any way, that it is all your responsibility? Alpha Males are highly logical. Handle it with logic.

First, ask for a discussion within a specific time frame. Go for a walk as you discuss the subject. Use notes if it helps you. Begin by a summary of the situation, calmly and in a friendly way, without a trace of rancor. Say, "There are eight steps to dinner, as I see it. *One,* plan what to have. *Two*, go to the market on the way home from work, or go on the weekend. *Three,* carry it home and put it away in the kitchen. *Four,* chop, mix, stir, fry, steam, or bake whatever it is. *Five,* put it on plates and take it to the table. *Six,* clear the dirty dishes away. *Seven*, wash them or load them into the dishwasher. *Eight*, put away the clean dishes in the cupboard. This adds up to a weekly contribution by me of x hours.

> *If you want to really make an Alpha Male happy, try saying to him the next time you have a disagreement, "We don't have to talk about this right now. Let's go get a pizza instead." This is a good tactic in any case. Although he is cut loose for now, he knows an exchange of views is in the air, and has time to adjust to the idea. Then when you gently ask for a few minutes of his undivided attention in a day or two, he is less likely to dig in his heels.*

"At my day job I earn a salary of $x. So my hourly wage is $y. Therefore at this rate, the time I spend preparing dinner seven days a week is worth $z. Since we both eat dinner on a regular basis, it seems to me that the cost in terms of time and work should be shared. So what do you prefer? Would you rather take on half the steps it takes each day (marketing, preparing, washing up, etc.) or would you like to do the whole job every other week? Or do you prefer to buy your way out by taking us out to dinner half of each week?"

Respect is essential to the Alpha Male. The best time to make a positive personal comment is when it is least expected. Even if you are in a discussion of deep disagreement, find one thing you truly admire about your Alpha Male. And say it. Then continue making your points of discussion.

When he vetoes one idea, present the others one by one in a calm, friendly way. Show him the list of labor-saving devices you will need (hot pot etc). If he vetoes those, present a list of his favorite meals and tell him what it will cost for your friend to prepare and deliver them. Keep the discussion positive and friendly. Even if your Alpha Male growls a bit, he will see the logic of it.

However, here comes an important point. *Do not try to get agreement right now.* Don't push him into a corner. Just say, "Well, let's mull over these ideas a bit if that's all right with you." But don't, at this stage, require him to *admit* that he sees the logic of it. Just make your points and let the thought mature in his mind.

Do not immediately require an Alpha Male to admit that he sees the logic of your argument. Just make your points and let the thought mature in his mind for a day or two. In dog training, you get your point across, then stop. You don't poke a stick in a dog's face if you hope to see him wag his tail.

Let a day or so go by, then proceed with the plan. Keep your manner very low-key. Tell him that you are planning meals and want to get his favorites, so which things would he like? Give him some prompts for things you know he likes and tell him that your friend will deliver them as soon as you and he choose what to get. Tell him the cost per meal and the cost per week. Tell him the dollar amount of his contribution, and that you will do all the arranging except for this. Give him figures for the cost of paying for the same meal at a restaurant. Let him think over all the elements of your point of view.

Then, begin to ease into the new plan with as little fuss as possible. Tell him you'll need a check from him each week for what you need. If you get about eighty-five percent of what you want, consider it a win.

Alpha Males make up for shortcomings in performance of domestic chores by extraordinary feats of achievement in areas involving strength, speed, endurance, and courage, especially under extreme or dangerous conditions. They also often earn more money (of course the inequality of pay for comparable jobs works in favor of most males and against most females in the United States at the rate of about three to two). So let your Alpha Male buy his way out of working hands-on at daily chores. If the net result is less work for you, it may work very well as a plan. Keep your eye on the overall picture and don't get lost in the details. Even if this aspect of your life is not an exactly-divided fifty-fifty proposition, if you can live with it, do; your Alpha Male will deliver more than his share in areas more attuned to his nature.

Ipse Dixit
ALPHA MALES IN THEIR OWN WORDS

"In recent years in the United States, there has been a movement by many women to attempt to alter fundamentally the way men think and feel. This too shall pass! Men have been men and acted as what they are for millions of years. Some cultures – the French, for instance – celebrate the differences between men and women instead of battling them. They even have a saying: Vive la difference!' *It may be worthwhile to consider this point of view".*

At some point any woman contemplating life as an equal partner with an Alpha Male of the human variety should consider the following question: Do you want *results* (that is, getting what you need in terms of a happy partner, a happy home, the strength and loyalty of an Alpha Male added to your own strengths) – or do you want to argue and confront him head-on in an attempt to change him to become like you and to feel as you do?

If you want a happy life with an Alpha Male, you have to allow him to be what he is. It *is* possible for a woman to take pride in the final result — a happy and contented partner — while doing such politically incorrect things as coddling, encouraging, and behaving in a gentle manner to her Alpha Male. Does this mean you end up with the short end of the stick? Does it mean you are subservient? A doormat? No, on the contrary, you expect and demand equality. But what he delivers and what you deliver are two different things. Equal and identical do not necessarily mean the same thing.

> *Why do most males behind the wheel of a car try to run down other men on bicycles? (They don't actually do it, but you can tell what they're thinking.) It's because bicycle riders appear to them to be vulnerable and therefore inferior. The man in the car sees himself as an Alpha Male, at least for the moment.*
>
> *However, true Alpha Males are less tempted by bicycle-riding targets because they have so many other ways to express real Alpha Male power. (And keep in mind that one of the greatest competitors in history won the most grueling bicycle race in the world, the Tour de France, multiple times even after being temporarily sidelined by cancer).*

It will doubtless be argued to the end of time whether men *could* feel and perceive and act as women do if they only tried harder. Or that women can and should become just as dominant and aggressive in the workplace as men. That men and women should share absolutely every chore equally — "I change the diaper, you change the next diaper." Our thoughts on this: Why bother?

As regards the workplace, everyone must be entitled by law to take whichever course each person decides on. The compensation must be the same for equal work. But it makes much more sense to preserve the differences inherent in men and women – don't start screaming, please – and divide up household chores in ways that capitalize on respective strengths of men and women. These vary considerably from case to case.

Routine chores are hard for Alpha Males. If alone and left to his own devices, an Alpha Male probably would not do these chores at all. Dishes pile up in the sink? No problem, there are always paper plates, or no plates (just eat while standing over the sink). Dust balls all over the floor? No problem, you won't trip over them. No clean sheets? No one ever died from sleeping on top of the quilt.

> *Here's the stark reality: If you think you can change a male – how he thinks, feels, and approaches life – you are doomed to disappointment. Yes, you can train him – that is, change his behavior in certain ways under certain conditions – but it is utterly impossible to change the way he is fundamentally constructed. He is, after all, different from you. He is a male, not a female. His role in life does not include carrying and bearing children. His own characteristics are just as hardwired and immutable as yours.*

As with all training, you get the best results if you train to bring out the best characteristics of the Alpha Male, whether canine or human, rather than dwelling too long on areas that are harder to develop because they do not come naturally to the beast. Hire someone part-time to do the household chores he doesn't want to do himself. If this doesn't fit your fiscal economic plan, trade the time it takes for you to do some of his share by requiring an exchange of his time to do something you want, say, taking a trip, getting the car serviced, putting in a fence, or raking the yard.

What to do if your Alpha Male shows his fangs.

You can, indeed you *must*, succeed in putting your views across without either losing your place of equality with your Alpha Male (he won't respect you if he can intimidate you) or having a confrontational argument. So, how do you go about it? Especially if he is snarling at you?

> *In dogs and wolves, there is a division in the upper lip (just below the nose) that enables the lips to be drawn far back to expose all the teeth, allowing the predator to take a good big bite out of an adversary or prey. In humans, a vestigial remnant of this same characteristic remains – the narrow indentation or channel that runs between the middle of the upper lip to just under the nose. Vestigial emotions probably remain as well.*

If your Alpha Male uses the tactic of bellowing or growling, look determined and do not smile. Keep cool and calm and logical. Speak slowly. Don't get rattled. Do not raise your voice. Do *not* say "Let me finish" – this will only put his hackles up further; he may wait, but he won't be listening to you while he does it. He will be waiting for the exact moment you stop talking to launch into the arguments he has been resentfully rehearsing in his mind ever since you said "Let me finish."

> *Every single day, find one thing you truly admire about your Alpha Male and tell it to him. Don't expect him to 'know' you think it. Males are not generally good at reading faces. They may not even 'know' you are thinking anything at all unless you tell them. Say it in words. Saying it in actions is even better. Alpha Males, being men of action, like physical contact.*

Instead, if you are interrupted or he talks while you are speaking, *repeat what you said as long as he talks over you.* Say something along these lines:

"Either we are on the same team or we're not. If we are, you have to show respect, even if you think I'm wrong. If I'm wrong, I'll change my position. You may be right, but you can't yell at me to tell me so. I won't accept it."

Or

"Don't try to intimidate me because I won't stand for it. I'm your *wife (girlfriend, partner).* Treat me accordingly. I'll understand what's bugging you if you can say it in words. If not, write it down. If not that, we can pay someone (a counselor) to help translate it into words for us."

Or

"We do different things in this partnership. I'm better at some of them, you're better at some of them. But I am an Alpha Female and don't ever forget it. Together we are one strong unbeatable team. I am every bit your equal."

Or this argument, which greatly appeals to most Alpha Males:

"You may be an Alpha Male, but I'm an Alpha Female. If you disrespect me, other people will disrespect me. This means they will be saying, 'Your wife (girlfriend) isn't so great.' *Therefore they will disrespect you, too."*

Or this argument, which appeals to his sense of honor (these are very high stakes):

"I took you for better or worse, richer or poorer, in sickness or in health, and I meant every word of it. If you are breaking your solemn, holy vow, I won't think very highly of you. We committed to become an inseparable team. If you tear me down, you tear down yourself."

<u>Growling over money.</u>

Some of the worst arguments arise over money. If you disagree with your Alpha Male, tell him:

"Show me the numbers." Ask for them in written form. Look them over carefully, asking for explanations. Listen to what he says. Speak in a slow, measured way. Even if you disagree with his conclusions, *repeat his version back to him* (but don't make it sound as if you are parroting) *so he knows you understand his view.* Then, and only then, make your points that differ from his.

> *When John D. Rockefeller first married, he told his young wife that he expected her to keep a notebook in which she must document every penny she spent on the household. This, he explained, would be an exercise in careful management of the household, but it would also be, he assured her, deeply interesting for her to know where each and every penny was spent.*
>
> *She sweetly (and immediately) put him straight about this idea. "No, John, I will not do that. I will manage our home with care and discretion, but I will do it as I think right."*
>
> *John D. backed off.*

When your Alpha Male meets you head-on with an outright refusal to do what you want, use this tactic: *Repeat what you just said.* You can change the word order or the words slightly, but say exactly the same thing, over and over. Use up your whole seven minutes (or whatever you stipulated when you began the discussion). Do this in a conversational tone, without showing so much as a trace of anger, frustration, annoyance, or even letting it become apparent that you are well aware that you are saying the same thing more than once. Make it sound, by your tone, that with each thing you repeat, you have come up with a whole new idea.

If your Alpha Male says "You said that already! Enough!" simply say, with absolute calm, "This is very, very important to me." Repeat as needed.

Don't nag – ever.

Once your specified time is up, stop talking.

Leave him alone to let the discussion mature in his mind. *To say more is to nag, and this is the most counterproductive mistake you can make.* Change the subject; suggest something comforting, like food or drink. Do not continue to talk about, or even allude to, the discussion. Go away for a time. Say: "Here's some pie / ice cream / rib roast. I'm going for a walk / to the gym / to see my aunt. See you in a couple of hours." This ends discussion on a comforting and unthreatening note.

> *Nagging never works. It makes your chances of winning a disagreement less favorable, not more. Make your points within the exact time you specified at the outset of the discussion, then stop. Do not so much as allude to the disagreement until the next scheduled discussion.*

What makes Alpha Males so slow to accept a different point of view?

Remember to allow your Alpha Male enough time to come around to a different point of view. In the wild (with wolves, for instance) the very survival of the Alpha Male, and hence of his pack, depends on the Alpha Male's having made the right decision based on his instinctive and immediate perceptions. If he's wrong, the whole pack, himself included, can be wiped out. All Alpha Males share this deep-seated characteristic. Changing his view is a dangerous matter, fraught with untold consequences. If he's wrong, he may be annihilated, along with everybody he cares about. Keep this in mind when trying to change an Alpha Male's views about something. Because he is logical, you can appeal to this. Remember to give him enough time for logic to overcome the weight of his entrenched position.

In order to lead his group safely, an Alpha Male needs to ponder his choices, and if you have presented him with a new choice, which he did not himself make, it will take him time to consider it from the standpoint of its implications for the safety of his pack. This behavior is deeply rooted in the Alpha Male's way of being. He needs time to come to agreement with you.

If the discussion ended inconclusively, let some time go by – a day or a week if possible. Set another meeting with a time limit. Keep it short, less than ten minutes, just long enough to present your points.

Training your Alpha Male with dog treats.

With dog training, it often helps to have some tasty dog snacks on hand for judicious dispensation. These can be used to encourage and reward good behavior, although they must never be used as a substitute for correction. The correct sequence is *Correction, Compliance, Dog Snack.*

Food is of great importance and is a great comforter to most Alpha Males. Remember the lines in the Beatles song, "Will you still need me, will you still feed me, when I'm sixty-four?"

Alpha Male humans have their own snack preferences, but the principle is the same.

Special treats and coddling can take many forms. Among the strangest Alpha Male phenomena is the craving, that lopsided yearning, many Alpha Males have for owning a boat. This generally takes the form of needing a powerboat, or of finding it necessary to make a single-handed trans-atlantic crossing in a sailboat. If your Alpha Male needs a boat for complete happiness, consider this his preferred method of coddling and go along for the ride. Even if you hate boats. Remember the Albatross (the Ancient Mariner killed the innocent and beautiful creature from angst at being stuck on a boat with no water, and then felt guilty about it for the rest of his life).

Some useful tactics in training.

When training your Alpha Male, here are some handy tactics to use as incentives and rewards. As you make your discussion points, consider using one or another of the following tactics:

- *Repackage* (add appealing side-attractions).

- *Reposition* (add other advantages to him).

- *Rethink* (decide if you can concede some part of your preferred course of action).

- *Humor* (say what you want in such a way as to get a laugh or at least a smile).

- *Get around "no"* (by changing the name of the request).

- *Postpone* and try again (present the same reasoning at a time when your Alpha Male is relaxed and happy, but only if you can hold an agreed-upon meeting within a fixed time-frame).

Here are some examples of how this could work:

- *Repackage:* (Add treats.)

  "On the way to my parents' house is a restaurant your friend Joe told us has great crab cakes. Why don't we stop there on the way?"

- *Reposition:* (Show special advantages to the Alpha Male.)

  "I've found out that there's a fantastic golf course near the headquarters of your new job on the West Coast, if you end up taking it. I looked into membership fees, and we could probably afford it. The web site says that the golf pro you told me about gives clinics there."

- *Rethink*: (See if you can let go of some part of your original proposal.)

  "It sure would be fun spending our wedding trip in Australia. There is great fishing off the Great Barrier Reef. If you don't want to go so far, what about Bermuda?"

- *Add humor*: (Say it in such a way as to get a laugh or at least a smile.)

  "Congratulations! For your birthday you've just won a chance to lift all my parents' heavy Victorian furniture."

- *Get around "no"* (by changing the name of the request.)

  "Any idea what it would cost to pay for a mover to help me move my parents' heavier items like the cabinets and computer station? I just can't quite make them budge."

- *Postpone*: (Do something else now — a pizza? a ballgame? — and try again later.) Let a day or two go by before you call another discussion.

These examples are meant as a general guide only. Workable solutions vary greatly with each situation, of course. But one or another can usually help you gain some degree of cooperation.

<u>What works: (What you *should* do) – a reminder.</u>

The point is, be flexible and be creative. Use the tools of Repackaging, Repositioning, Rethinking, Changing the name of the request, Postponement, and Humor to get what you want. Throw in an honest compliment when you can, especially when it is least expected. Use logic. Keep meetings short and within a specified time. Stop mid-sentence if necessary to remain strictly within the time limit. Walk with, don't sit facing, your Alpha Male while you have discussions. Quit when you sense that the message has actually entered the Alpha Male's brain. Don't push for immediate outright agreement. If things ended inconclusively, let at least a day or, better still, a week go by before you call the next meeting.

<u>What doesn't work: (What you should *never* do).</u>

Do not scold, nag, or confront. None of these will work. You can't win all the time, but you can win some of the time. And as

> *Remember, confrontation is his turf. He's very good at it. So don't play that game.*

you train your Alpha Male, he will probably become marginally *less* prone to dig in his heels in opposition because he will find that you *don't* confront him.

<u>Sharing your innermost feelings with an Alpha Male.</u>

Here is a subject that many women married to Alpha Males — and some who are considering marrying one and are already hard at work training him — complain about. They want to discuss a problem that is important to them, generally one involving something in the relationship they have with their Alpha Male, and they are met with absolute and obstinate stonewalling.

> *Insisting on discussions of your innermost feelings with your Alpha Male upsets him; it gives him a feeling that his safe haven is falling apart. Therefore he will have no place to come home to and lick his wounds, be coddled and fed and restored, in order to be able to go out again to do battle on behalf of his pack. The world is a dangerous place. Discussion of things wrong with his safe haven threatens his very existence, and that of his pack.*

Not only does he not want to discuss it, he will do practically anything to get out of even having the subject mentioned. His response may be anything from silence to anger to absence. If cornered, he will blow you off with a joking remark, or listen in a distracted or sullen way and make no effort to get at the problem under discussion.

There is only one thing to say about this tendency many women have to discuss their emotional concerns, insecurities, or thoughts on the state of their relationship with their Alpha Male: The word is, *Don't.*

Alpha Males don't want to tell you their innermost feelings, and they don't want to hear about your innermost feelings either. They are simple creatures really. They want an orderly life without emotional complications. If you need to share your innermost feelings, find a woman friend, or a non-Alpha Male friend who likes pondering puzzles of this nature.

> *Alpha Males are warriors, men of action, leaders. They don't want to be anything else. Sharing their innermost feelings is absolutely the last thing they want to do. Think about it: In the wild, a wolf who shared his innermost feelings with another wolf would probably get eaten while doing so, or another wolf would find out what his innermost feelings were and organize an attack on him and his women and children while the first wolf was still describing his inner wolf cub.*

A tale of two Alpha Males.

[Please note: This behavior is actually against the law, and we do not recommend anyone do the same sort of thing.]

Tom wanted to marry Angela. Angela set him a task. Angela's sister lived in Washington, D.C., three hours' drive away. The sister was continually being harassed by a former boyfriend who had used her for a punching bag. Nothing the sister did could make her ex-boyfriend leave her alone. Tom's task was to make the ex-boyfriend stop, once and for all.

Tom called his brother, Jack, who lived close by. "I'd like to kill that SOB," Tom told his brother. "I need you to come down to D.C. with me tomorrow to stop him for good." The next morning the two took the train, paying cash for the tickets. They rented a car, paying cash. No one knew they were in town and they had left no paper trail.

They knew from Angela that the ex-boyfriend worked as a postman, and what his route was. They drove around for an hour or two before they spotted him in his postal jeep. For an hour or more they followed the jeep in their rented car. The jeep at last turned onto a quiet side street.

Finally the culprit got out of the jeep, leaving the driver's-side door open. He walked around and opened the back of the jeep and threw in his mail sack. Tom and Jack got a good look at him. No one was around. Their moment had come.

Tom pushed his foot to the floor. The rental car sped forward. The impact took the jeep door cleanly off its hinges. Tom said later, "Let me put it to you this way: It wasn't closeable any more." It lay in the street yards away.

Then the two brothers pulled up as though they were going to inspect this terrible accident. They stepped out of the rented car and walked toward the jeep.

The culprit, who had watched all this happen from behind the mail jeep, came steaming over. "How dare you do this! You idiots! You're nuts!" he screamed at them. It was clear he had no idea who they were.

Tom looked at him calmly. "Boy," he drawled slowly, "it's lucky you weren't standing there. You could have been <u>seriously hurt</u>."

At that point, Tom stepped close to the culprit and 'stood over' him, invading his space without actually touching him. "If you ever go anywhere near Angela's sister again, you <u>will</u> be seriously hurt," he said very quietly.

Tom and his brother got back into their rented car with the smashed headlight and drove away. (They later explained to the rental company that Washington, D.C. was certainly hazardous to drive around in.)

This is a fairly typical Alpha Male response to a challenge: He figures out what needs to be done, achieves the objective, and generally has a good time doing it. Where lesser males might look for intermediaries to do the face-to-face confrontation, an Alpha Male is not only unafraid of direct confrontation, he actually is good at it and even thrives on it.

"It was worth the money when that SOB figured out who we were," Tom said later.

Alpha Males need to know that they are superior to other males. They need to prove it not only to their pack, but if challenged, before the whole world.

9.

THE ALPHA MALE AT WORK: WHERE ALPHA MALES RULE

This chapter is essential reading if you want to understand fully the Alpha Male and his connection with the workplace, because an Alpha Male _is_ his job. He cannot be separated from it. Alpha Males control most corporations and non-profit organizations (with a few notable exceptions). You need to understand both how the corporations operate, and how the Alpha Male functions in them, so you can make an informed choice whether to compete yourself against the Alpha Males who dominate corporations, or choose to marry an Alpha Male and let him compete for you.

Ipse Dixit
ALPHA MALES IN THEIR OWN WORDS

"There's a man who has collected all kinds of Army tanks – actual U.S. Army tanks and personnel carriers. They operate, but all their guns and cannons are disabled. You can pay a few thousand dollars and go to his ranch out West and ride around in these tanks. He shows you how to operate them. Corporations are bringing their sales forces – their guys – to let them drive around in them and play at war. Where do women fit into this?"

How does a woman fit into the male-dominated workplace? Can she compete equally with an Alpha Male on the job? Has the playing field been leveled at last for most women in the work world? This chapter is key to understanding the whole picture of life with an Alpha Male, because his job is the central piece of that picture. Ignore that, and you are only dealing with the fringes, not the core.

It raises this question: Is it a legitimate choice to decide *not* to enter the corporate (or nonprofit) workplace yourself, and to send in your Alpha Male to do battle for both of you? Is this somehow "selling out"? Are you turning back the clock to a time when women were not permitted to enter the workplace at all (at least, those of a certain class; no one ever said much about the women at the lowest rungs of the social hierarchy who drudged as charwomen, laborers, scullery maids, factory workers, and the like). Are you somehow retrograde if you decide to stay home and work at something you like or start your own business while creating a good and enjoyable life for your Alpha Male husband? (Should you at least feel guilty if you do?)

> *Wolves hunt for food and survival — even prosperity — but never kill more than they can eat. It is here that parallels to the wolf pack and the human Alpha Male in the workplace begin to diverge dramatically.*

The purpose of this chapter is to give you enough information so you can make an informed decision on how to structure your life with an Alpha Male to satisfy you both. Should you work in a corporation? Should you compete head-to-head with an Alpha Male? Should you avoid the structured corporate or nonprofit workplace altogether and head in an entirely different direction? Should your chosen Alpha Male compete in a corporation while you handle all other aspects of your life together outside this arena? This chapter addresses these and other questions.

Today, young women are being told that there is no job level to which they cannot rise; there is no field of work in which they cannot achieve and succeed on equal footing with males. They are simultaneously being told that they can 'have it all' — a high-power job, a husband, and a family — and lots of women are shocked and dismayed (and confused) to learn as time goes on that this is simply not so. With only token representation at the highest levels, most women work extremely hard, do everything they have been told to do to succeed (by the corporation or whatever), and ultimately, when they do not get promoted to or even near the top, finally drop out in discouragement. Some simply 'burn out.' The trouble is they are being sold a bill of goods.

Get ready: You may not like what you are about to hear about the Alpha Male, and others, in the workplace:

The working world is controlled by Alpha Males and is run for their benefit. If you are looking for a job in a corporation, you will have to confront this reality. Corporations are excellent places to observe the Alpha Males in action. Just don't get in their way if you don't want to get run over.

> *Ipse Dixit*
> **ALPHA MALES IN THEIR OWN WORDS**
>
> *"A corporation has only one purpose: to make money for shareholders. Excess capital is invested, providing jobs for the masses. For investors, return on capital is the only goal. There has never been another goal."*

In the wolf pack, the Alpha Male leads the hunt and protects his territory by driving off or killing off competitors. He directs other pack members in the hunt, positioning them strategically by silent gestures of his head and body. When the wolf pack kills, the Alpha Male eats his fill first, then the Beta wolf eats, and so on down to the lowest pack member, who gets whatever is left. The Alpha Female eats before any other female, and before any male she can intimidate.

The work world today is still, despite some small advances here and there, run by men, and run along the same lines as those of a hunting pack of wolves. There is, at best, lip service to the equality of men and women on the job, but women still earn sixty-nine cents on the dollar for the same jobs as men, and there is still no sign of an Equal Rights Amendment being passed in the United States, the most powerful and prosperous nation in the world.

> *Ipse Dixit*
> **ALPHA MALES IN THEIR OWN WORDS**
>
> *"If women do not make an equal contribution to the job — and many do not — why should they get equal pay? The men who don't contribute don't get paid well either."*

Corporations function exactly like a wolf pack. The top wolf gives orders to all others beneath him, and they do as they are told; they in turn order around those below them in the hierarchy. The only aim of the wolf pack is to bring home dinner. In corporations, dinner becomes money. But here is a small difference: Wolves don't become fanatical about bringing home immense dinners far larger than their pack can consume. They hunt for a balanced end-result – enough to provide for all the pack members: the hunters themselves and the females and young left behind during the hunt. With corporations, the true goal has been lost sight of. '*More'* is the only goal. The 'kill' goes to the (usually) Alpha Males who run the corporation, and to the stockholders. What scraps remain pay salaries of the workers.

In every realm of life, the Alpha Male feels driven to prove himself. There is no letup – he is a triumph of action over calm reflection. He *defines* himself by action and by his job. At the same time, he is driven relentlessly to protect his territory, whether it is his home, his family, or his job. This is the natural order of things for an Alpha Male. He sees aggression not as something unpleasant and unnecessary in the workplace, but as the way things ought to be, with himself at the top of the pile.

Ipse Dixit
ALPHA MALES IN THEIR OWN WORDS

"Aggression? No — competition and winning. People who only want to make enough money to have a good life, whether men or women, are not the driven persons that Alphas seek in their employees. Is this why men's work is valued more highly? Because most men are driven and most women are not?"

Without his work, without the possibility of taking decisive action (often courageous, sometimes risky and foolhardy), the Alpha Male feels diminished. If he isn't proud of himself, he will not be proud of anyone else, including his chosen female. Men *are* their jobs. They lose a sense of self and identity without it. Like it or not, in many ways his woman comes second to this essential need.

The Roman Senate assembled, just before the time of Christ, to hear firsthand of the brilliantly successful military campaign into what is present-day France by their most celebrated warrior, Julius Caesar. He stood before them and delivered his speech. It was exactly three words long: "Veni, vidi, vici." – I came, I saw, I conquered.

Alpha Males should all have this emblazoned as a motto on their T-shirts. It is the way they view the world. This is especially true of the way Alpha Males view the workplace.

A job for most women is a means to make enough money to live on, to give one the freedom to have a way of life that is pleasing, and a hedge against being broke in the future. For men, a job is almost entirely about winning. The road for Alpha Males at work is straight and narrow; the view on the way to winning the game is irrelevant. Alpha Males celebrate and feel happy as a result of having won, after it's all over.

Alpha Males *act*. They do what they want first, then justify their actions later if forced to do so. Risk and glory are concepts that draw the Alpha Male toward them and away from security and peace (this probably has a good deal to do with why we are still trying to settle differences by wars instead of discussion, although wars have never resolved any difference in the long run; the loser fuming with resentment until he can get in his licks at the one who beat him). This action-driven approach to solving problems also fuels the Alpha Male in the workplace.

Alpha Males know how to compete, how to try again and again, how use force in argument, how to intimidate, how to keep going until they win. As a group, they are often good at fistfights, at loud argument, at football, at war. They bring well-developed skills drawn from experience to the workplace.

Any weakness is impossible to tolerate, because a male's competitor will seize on it to destroy him. Therefore many men in the workplace actually despise women, whose more indirect approach to work (women are more likely to ask politely for something rather than demand it, for instance) they see as weakness. This is added to the fact that many men already think less of women for their comparative physical weakness. Any male who shows deference to a woman, even if the woman is right, even if she is his boss, even if he is going to ruin a project unless he bows to her will – is viewed by at least some males as weak. All this creates confusing crosscurrents in the workplace.

What a good many males, especially Alpha Males, really want is for women to stand by and see how strong, how brave, how decisive, how brilliant they are, and how thoroughly they win, leaving all competition sprawled in the mud at their feet, whimpering. These men want to be admired, noticed, and made to feel important for this.

Is this right? Should women have to play by these rules? Maybe not, but this is in fact what women face in the corporate workplace. Enter at your own risk.

On the trading floor of the New York Stock Exchange – a testosterone-fueled pit with perhaps more Alpha Males per square foot than anywhere else on earth — traders are nearly all men. They thrive on the adrenalin-rush pressure and are intent on one thing: grabbing for themselves the best outcome from every change.

Ipse Dixit
ALPHA MALES IN THEIR OWN WORDS

"Every change in the numbers is an opportunity. Second-rate guys are afraid of change. I love it because it gives me a chance to take something from a competitor on the [trading] floor."

A chief executive officer who takes a huge portion of the incoming money and perquisites for himself – a salary in the millions of dollars annually with free use of the corporate jet, for instance – and who arranges deals by which he walks away with scores of millions more if he should be ousted from his job — is not earning money. He is amassing an outsized pile to prove that he can. He may measure his pile against that of other Alpha Males. (Alpha Males love to measure absolutely everything, a trait that begins as early as they can stand side by side as small boys.) But its value as legal tender for life's necessities and luxuries is irrelevant. Genuine wolves stop eating when they have eaten their fill. Human ones don't.

Of course, this no longer works the way it once did. With all those CEOs walking off with nearly all the money, the remaining percentage to pay salaries has shrunk. With the wholesale shipping abroad of jobs that once formed the bedrock of salary-generating jobs (like manufacturing and the automobile industries to the Far East and information technologies jobs to

India), the rug has been jerked from beneath the feet of the average wage earner. What has all this to do with Alpha Males? It impacts the stress level in the workplace. If you choose to compete in the corporate workplace, you will have no way to avoid it.

> *Ipse Dixit*
> **ALPHA MALES IN THEIR OWN WORDS**
>
> *"Women in the workplace confuse me. I don't know whether to be protective of them as I instinctively want to be, or to obliterate them if they are competing with me. It breaks my focus and for that reason alone I think it's a bad idea. Men produce best when there are no distractions."*

Today, in many cases, *both* men and women have to work at full pace just to bring in the same income a man alone once brought home, which was then sufficient to provide for a family, educate the kids, and leave enough for an annual vacation. Unless a man — an Alpha Male usually — is a superior earner, a family needs two wage earners, not one, working full time just to maintain the way of life we term 'middle-class.' Competitiveness in the workplace is very great, due in part to this increased stress. If one of the family's earners is an Alpha Male, this stress may be considerably reduced; Alpha Males are usually excellent — even spectacular — earners.

Keep in mind that in most marriages the wife, in addition to her job outside the home, still does most of the work needed to run the household – cooking, cleaning, caring for babies or children, and all the rest. Consequently, you should ask yourself whether you want to work in a corporation as hard as a man does. If you do, it is a perfectly acceptable choice, as long as you get proper training and know what you are getting into. However, you will do virtually nothing else, and trying to juggle the commitments to children and family is not easy.

In a corporation, being male is an advantage. Being female in a corporation is a distinct disadvantage from the very start, no matter where you fit in the power structure. The well-known "glass ceiling" — an invisible point above which women seldom rise in corporations regardless of ability — is still very common, despite a handful of notable exceptions in recent years. Most women who rise to the number-one position in large corporations either inherited the company from their Alpha Male husband or started it themselves. Very few women are promoted to the helm.

Ipse Dixit
ALPHA MALES IN THEIR OWN WORDS

"Thousands of new corporations are started every year, almost all by men. Why aren't at least half of them started by women?"

It follows that many men who are less qualified than women hold jobs for which they are paid more than women. It is not difficult to find in most corporations men who get good salaries but are mediocre to poor at their jobs. This is not fair, but it is fact in many corporations. This is the game you are entering when you seek to work in a corporation.

Question: What do you call the medical student who is so dumb that he graduates at the very bottom of his class?

Answer: <u>Doctor</u>.

<u>Here's the point.</u>

If this doesn't appeal to you, you may want to send in your Alpha Male to compete in this particular arena. Either choice is valid. Just don't let corporations work a con job on you. It's a men's game, invented by men, played by men with a nearly three-to-two advantage against women in terms of compensation, and it is played by creatures who have spent their entire lives being male.

> *"Most men lead lives of quiet desperation"*
> *–Ralph Waldo Emerson*

There is nothing wrong with finding an Alpha Male, marrying him, and creating a calm, happy home life that allows him to charge into the fray instead of you, if you choose this route. His chances of success in the corporation are far better than yours.

Ipse Dixit
ALPHA MALES IN THEIR OWN WORDS

"Most women lead lives of <u>noisy</u> desperation."

<u>Why Alpha Males *must* earn money.</u>

All males like to measure things. From early childhood they are measuring, comparing, and drawing conclusions from their data. They then relate these conclusions to hierarchy. The bigger it is, the better you are for having it. The better you are, the higher you are on the totem pole as compared to other males. The higher you are on the totem pole, the more closely you resemble an Alpha Male. Alpha Males get to push everybody else around and they don't have to take orders form anybody. They're 'the man,' and everyone else pays attention when they speak and gets out of the way when they strut through. Who *wouldn't* want this? (Well, most women wouldn't; but virtually all would-be Alpha Males most assuredly would.)

When they get old enough to have a first summer job, these little males measure their success against that of their male friends – "My paper route / lemonade stand / dog-walking service makes more money than yours does. Therefore I am better than you."

In high-school sports – and sometimes in academics – young Alpha Males compete for honor and position, because generally there is no money involved. In graduate schools (they compete to get into the best) the competition becomes ferocious in many cases. And competition for first jobs follows the same pattern. If mine is bigger or better, then I'm more Alpha Male than you are.

> *"Winning isn't everything; it's the only thing."*
> *– Vince Lombardi, legendary football coach*

Money now becomes the measure of success. Money for Alpha Males and would-be Alpha Males is not, as it is for many women, a means of having some control over your life, of buying things, or a way to ensure security.

> *For males – especially Alpha Males – money is simply power, control, and status. If you have it, you have these three all-important things. If you have more of it, you have more power, control, and status. If you have so much money you cannot possibly even spend it, you're one hell of a guy.*

It's a good thing money was invented, from the Alpha Male point of view. It makes life nice and simple, so you can focus narrowly, as Alpha Males do, and simply go ahead in a straight line toward wealth. Money is so easy to measure, too. You just look at whose pile is bigger and no one has to argue. The big pile wins.

So it should come as no great surprise that Alpha Males in the working world move resolutely in a straight line toward gaining money. They naturally like moving in straight lines from A to B to C to D anyway. They are good at ignoring anything along the way. In fact, most males cannot easily follow more than one line of action at a time. They just like to move along as fast as possible toward that single goal: money.

Ipse Dixit
ALPHA MALES IN THEIR OWN WORDS

"Some men want money, some men want raw power. Money sometimes equals power, but not always."

When they have money, especially lots of it, they feel good. There it is, proof of their Alpha Male-ness. Money compensates, at least momentarily, for the uneasiness all males feel at some level – that of being almost irrelevant in the actual process of passing on their DNA to a future member of the species. Yes, women need men — but a particular man has no assurance of being the one whose genetic code will be carried forward. That is, unless he is an Alpha Male, and hence sufficiently intimidating to those shadowy lesser males (who are always circling the camp just out of sight both day and night) to keep them away from the Alpha Male's chosen female.

Ipse Dixit
ALPHA MALES IN THEIR OWN WORDS

"Part of being an Alpha Male is the feeling that you can do anything, you can achieve anything, you can accomplish anything. If you read, you study, you work, you put in the time, you can do anything."

Women should not be surprised by the ruthlessness shown by males in the workplace, both to other males and usually to any female ignorant or audacious enough to challenge them. What you're doing by competing with him is telling a male (by your action if not words) that when he dies, he is extinct for eternity. At some level a male knows you don't 'need' a big pile of money in the same way he does – that is, for the purpose of driving off competitors for his one chance at immortality through being certain that *his* DNA is passed on to the next generation. Here you are, competing with him for something you don't really need, while he really does need it. He resents your competing with him even if he's not conscious of the reason. Sound far-fetched? It's not.

> *"The most important thing: Tell the truth. Don't lie. Be as tough as you need to be. The business world is a man's world. Don't ever forget it. No matter how good a job you do, you're always going to be from a foreign country."*
> — *A successful businesswoman*

An Alpha Male talks about his work.

"Okay. I admit it. I am an Alpha dog. A wolf.

"What do I do for a living? I hunt. I run a corporation and I make a lot of money. I am The Boss. The Big Dog. The Man. The Alpha. I can't help it; I was born that way.

"And so I hunt. I hunt a lot. I win. I am rich. The chair at the head of the table is set for me. Everyone follows my orders. I follow no one.

"I have a wife and kids and a beautiful house and sports cars and a lot of very expensive stuff. I love my wife and children. I am loyal, trustworthy, chivalrous, and very protective of my family. It would not be a stretch to say that I would lay down my life for them. My wife is a successful professional. My kids are leaders at their schools. That I respect them is essential. I also like sex, food, and quiet reading time in the bathroom. My home is my den where I rest up.

"I'm told a lot of women pursue other guys like me. But they'd better be careful what they wish for. I am an enormous ego driving a steamroller at high speed with no brakes on a one-way highway. I would suggest not getting in the way. That is just the way it is.

"I do not come from money and I had no connections. But I did fight my way into getting an Ivy League education and have spent untold hours learning the tools of my trade. I work endless hours. When I first joined the company I saw the boardroom. Mahogany-paneled walls. Long marble table. Leather chairs. I knew that the chair at the head of the table would be mine. It is.

"Of late there are distractions at work. These are called women. A woman manager comes into my office to report — I have undressed her with my eyes. I can't help it; it's just the way it is. Is it fair to expect me to also be listening to what she says? There are all kinds of rumblings and buzzings about glass ceilings, equal pay, maternity leave, childcare. Who cares? These are my hunting grounds. Women do not belong here. They are not part of my hunting pack. They are not team players. I want to hunt with men who have no other life outside their job — or if they do, fine, but keep it to themselves; I don't give a damn about it. This is my turf. It is my hunt. I have big teeth and I will eat anyone who gets in my way.

"Does this sound uncivilized and primitive?

"I told you I was a wolf."

<u>Why males who have inherited wealth are almost never Alpha Males.</u>

Most men who have inherited great wealth do not have to earn money. Two things happen as a result.

First, they do not learn the skills needed to earn money. They do not learn the way to 'go out there and get some more money' as others do. A kind of panic can set in: "I have a lot of inherited money, but if I were to lose it, I wouldn't know how to go about earning more. I'd be helpless."

Second, many men with inherited wealth feel a sort of guilt at having inherited money with no real reason other than that they happened to be born to the father who had the fortune before them. They can feel quite diminished, and comments like "He's sure not the man his father was" can be painful.

Males, even those who in other circumstances might have developed as Alpha Males, are put in the role of being caretakers of their fortune rather than earners. Although some become good at this, and manage the money well, such males can feel inadequate (although they would never admit it). Forming a foundation to give some of their wealth away is often the best they can do to create a role for themselves in which they are 'in charge' and 'the boss.' There's nothing wrong with this, and some foundations do a great deal of good, but the men who do this are seldom Alpha Males. They can never shake the feeling that they could lose their money forever, or that some tougher male could accuse them, rightly, for having simply walked into a fortune and not gone out and got it for himself, like any self-respecting Alpha Male.

<u>The pros and cons of having an office romance.</u>

Do the advantages of an office romance outweigh the downside? Almost never. However tempting a romance may be, it gets in the way of the simple rules of the wolf-pack setup of a corporation or nonprofit organization. Males are confused about how to treat females – should they protect them as one aspect of their maleness directs them? Or obliterate them if they dare to compete? To an already complicated situation it adds another confusing dimension. Males are feeling threatened also by the fact that women are *competing at all* for money, the male's single measure of his own worth in many cases.

Add to this confusing mix a personal relationship, with trust and generosity and mutual helpfulness, and throw the resulting mixture into the existing structure of the wolf pack, and you create a dangerous morass. What does a male do if the hierarchy tells him to do something that will harm his romantic partner? Which wins out, the rules of the game or the rules of love? These rules are highly different and nearly entirely incompatible.

If you do fall in love, one of you may be well advised to move to another company, or at the very least, to a department with little or no connection with that of your partner. The safest rule, however, with regard to office romances, is: <u>Don't</u>.

<u>Setting your sights on marrying the boss: How to go about it (and when *not* to).</u>

If you are sufficiently attractive (this has little to do with your actual looks, more to do with your style of dress, speech, movement, and sometimes your social class) and you think you could make a good wife for the boss, then reread Chapters 2 through 6 before you begin your campaign. You might also review the points made earlier about the risks inherent in any interoffice romantic attachment.

The one unchangeable point: If he is married, don't do it. No excuse is good enough. He may be in a bad marriage, his wife may cheat on him, he may be making eyes at you on a daily basis. But married men are off limits, period. And not for the reason alone that cheating anyone is a sleazy thing to do.

The old saying that *"a man who marries his mistress leaves a job opening"* is true. If he cheats with you now, he may cheat against you later.

Further, if he marries you, after having cheated with you while married, part of him will always think that you could do the same thing to him. Part of him will think less of you for having cheated with him; although he will never say it, he will think you are not quite the first-rate woman he was after. And, above all, *he will think less of himself* for having 'settled for' a second-rate woman. And he will blame this on you.

But if your boss is fair game and you work for him but really want to be married to him, how do you go about it? If you work for an Alpha Male, you are in his company a lot. How do you get his attention in the workplace, and get him to ask you out, leading to marriage?

There are no guarantees, of course, but here are some rules of engagement:

First and most important: Do not 'notice' him. Do not appear to know he exists as a man. Keep your behavior and your focus strictly on your work; perform your job extremely well. If he thinks you have 'noticed' him and are interested in him, he may show you interest in return, but it is not this kind of interest that you want. This kind of interest (simply his responding to your already-expressed interest in him) will not – repeat *not* – set the stage for eventual marriage. He may ask you out. But the process will be on the wrong track from day one. He will feel he already owns you.

Second: Do not 'chase' him. Remember that Alpha Males *have to pursue.* They are constructed this way. Everything they do that has value to them requires pursuit. Why? Because an Alpha Male has to feel that he alone can triumph where lesser men fail. What comes easily, an Alpha Male does not value. He must achieve the (nearly) impossible so that he feels validated ("I got the unattainable. No other man could have done it. Therefore I'm one hell of a guy").

> *"All things that are, are with more spirit chased than enjoyed"*
> —*William Shakespeare*

Third: Dress well and have a good haircut and attractive makeup (most Alpha Males prefer a light touch that gives the effect, to them, of 'no makeup'). Develop a low-pitched pleasant speaking voice (high-pitched voices and laughter annoy many males). Speak slowly and with deliberation – it makes you sound as if you know more than you are saying. Excitable voices don't benefit you. Alpha Males find them irritating in most cases.

Once you have set the stage, either he will notice you and find you attractive, or he will not. Give him enough time. And be sure you continue doing interesting things outside of the office — a sport, charity work, tutoring a child or adult, sailing a boat, raising racing pigeons, writing a book, studying Swahili, making a documentary movie — and let him hear about it indirectly, either through a co-worker or by photographs casually left on the copy machine. If he's interested, he'll pick up on it. If he isn't, forget it. Pursuing him will *not* work. Move on.

A genuine Alpha Male loves to overcome challenges. If you are not available even to him, he knows you are not available to anyone lesser. Therefore he will value you even more. If he is on the level, he will propose marriage properly at the proper time, and he will feel like the luckiest man in the world because he won a prize not attainable to anyone but himself. This makes him feel pleased *with himself*, without which no marriage can succeed at the highest level.

If it looks as if he is in love with you and actually tells you he wants to marry you, but wants a physical relationship now, don't do it. Stick to your resolve.

The true story of competition between a happily married Alpha Male and his Alpha Female wife:

They are in their middle fifties. He's a prominent medical doctor; she's an attorney with a well-regarded law firm. They are clearly in love with each other after thirty years of marriage, and both are at the top of their game in their respective professions. Something about them reminds you of Nick and Nora Charles in *The Thin Man* movies. They joke, they are respectful of one another, they like being around each other. But being true examples of the Alpha, they are highly competitive. The attorney wife tells the story:

> *"This happened when we were in our early forties. At dinner we'd talk in front of the children about my law practice, or how things were going at my husband's medical practice, because these were both businesses we individually owned. I'm not sure if the children first raised the question of which of us earned the most money. It was summertime, July or August, when the topic came up, and I said, because I'm a very competitive person, 'Let's have a contest. Let's see who can earn more money this year.'*

> *"The children were positively gleeful at this idea that mom and dad were going to have a contest. As*

the year progressed, the children would periodically ask us 'Who is winning?' and I'd say 'This is how much I brought in so far this year,' and my husband would say, 'This is how much I've brought in'.

"As we approached the year-end deadline, I was ahead, and my husband clearly was a little bit distressed by this. So, in October of that year, he changed his billing practices. Instead of billing every thirty days, he suddenly was billing every fifteen days, bringing the capital that ordinarily would have come in the following year forward into the year of the contest. And in the end, he won. I was mad. And I've never forgotten it." *(She is, however, laughing and shaking her head in mock disbelief as she says it.)*

They are not competitive in all areas, however. "How do I make my Alpha Male happy?" asks the wife. "I make his life interesting. That means in every aspect of his life, including the sexual aspect. Men are very simple. He and I have always had our separate careers. When I came home at night, I had my stories to tell, he had his stories to tell. I organize his life where he wants me to, and he does the same for me. I take care of social engagements, for instance; he does most of the planning for our trips, with the children when they were at home, and for us both now they're grown. "

The son of two Alphas tells how his parents' work-styles differ.

"My father worked incredibly hard to get to the top and didn't care about the hours he worked. My mom decided she wanted to be an attorney, and she went and did what was necessary to do it; she didn't care that women weren't attorneys at that time. But she decided that she didn't like certain jobs, or she didn't like certain hours, so she

wouldn't work crazy hours because she didn't want to. She wouldn't do divorce cases because they weren't interesting to her. It didn't matter how much they paid. This is a big difference between men and women. A man in the same position would have different goals. He would do exactly what he's supposed to do to succeed the most. Even if he hated divorce cases, he'd grind them out just like everything else, and he'd work the long hours; this is a major difference between how most men and women approach a job."

"You have a project with a deadline: you assign it to a team of four men. They spend the first two days figuring out who reports to whom on the team."
"You assign the same project to a team of four women: they jump in, finish the job in a few hours, and go on to the next project. Or maybe to lunch.

Alpha Males speak about the workplace.

- *"A good example of the problems women have in the workforce is this: Look at the way people fight. If a man fights with another man, there are rules of engagement. When women fight with other women, there are no rules. They'll do anything at all. They don't fight fair like we do."*

- *When my boss says something to me, it's not how he says it, it's what he says."*

- *"I did not get to the top [of my field] by leaving bodies strewn around, by being cunning and devious and cutting out other people. I got to the top by studying hard and working very, very hard, long hours, and making myself necessary, getting the job done, so that when positions became available, the upper management would naturally turn to me. I gradually got one promotion after another, by just plain working like a dog. I had focus, set my sights, and did what I had to do in terms of gaining the knowledge, skills, and ability to do the job."*

- *"Men, and Alpha Males in particular, are risk-takers. In fact, it's an essential feature of the Alpha Male that he takes risks. Women in general are not risk-takers. If you look at the graduating class of a medical school, it's the man who's going to go into debt, open an office, hire a staff, try to make a go of his own practice, and try to make a lot of money, which he often does. The graduating women will get the medium-paying staff nine-to-five job and be quite satisfied with it, and never take the risk of starting her own practice."*

- *"A man can be called out to fight, and this is always in the back of a guy's head. What do you do in a bar if a guy says, 'Let's you and I step outside'? He has said, 'Now we are going to solve our differences. We're not going to the authorities with this, but we're going to engage. Let's go.' You never lose the knowledge that if you start trouble you are going to have to finish it."*

- *"The reason men don't work in nonprofit organizations is because these are about idealism and charity, which are not masculine concepts. Nonprofits are not enough about winning."*

> *"If you find a dog in the gutter, and raise him up and feed him, he will not bite you. This is the principal difference between a dog and a man."*
> *— Mark Twain*

- *"As far as a law firm is concerned, all that counts is the lawyer that puts out the most billable hours. It doesn't matter how smart or effective their work is — did they put in twenty hours a day? Did they bill two thousand or three thousand hours a year? That's the bottom line and that's the only thing that counts."*

- *"When a guy says something to me, he means what he says, and I'm not there to pick up the nuance of his tone. I don't care. And I don't need to know. But I've learned from being with women that I need to pay attention. I don't actually pay attention a lot more, but I listen to what they paid attention to, and I've learned that these things are important to them."*

Ipse Dixit
ALPHA MALES IN THEIR OWN WORDS

"Washington, D.C. is a city of six thousand future Presidents."
—William P. Goodwin, Chief Counsel to U.S. Senators Sam Ervin (d, NC) and Sam Nunn (d, GA)

ALPHA MALES IN THEIR OWN WORDS

"Why I think women do poorly in corporate America:

1. This is men's turf. Always has been. No one gives up turf without a fight.

2. Women are disruptive in the workplace. They are sex objects to most males.

3. Women don't play by the rules. It has been a man's game, so men get to make the rules.

4. Women are not driven to work as hard as men. They do not <u>become</u> their jobs, as men do.

5. Women do not seek the power that men seek. They won't put in the hours men do to gain power.

6. Most men are prejudiced against women in the workplace.

7. Women are not team players.

8. They are not Alpha Males.

The bottom line for Alpha Males is:

<u>*Power*</u>
<u>*Energy*</u>
<u>*Number One*</u>
<u>*Intelligence*</u>
<u>*Success*</u>

Read it top to bottom and you'll see what us Alpha Males are really measuring."

10.

KEYS POINTS
TO REMEMBER

Here are the key points to remember in your pursuit of happiness with an Alpha Male. Consult these for a review of your strategy for finding, marrying, and training an Alpha Male who will be a worthy partner in a happy marriage with you.

- Alpha Males are not for everyone. Be sure you want one.

- An Alpha Male is decisive and commanding. It is his nature to be like this. You have to train him to listen to your point of view.

- Alpha Males are actually not all that difficult to understand. Despite the fact that they are often highly intelligent, high-energy men driven to succeed, they operate in a very simple, straightforward way.

- An Alpha Male may try to dominate you. Give respect and demand respect from him. Love dies without it.

- Loyalty is the bedrock of life with an Alpha Male. Without loyalty, nothing good can follow. Give one-hundred percent; demand one-hundred percent.

- If your Alpha Male tries to encroach on you, stand your ground. Confront him with logic. Other kinds of confrontation will not work.

- Call a scheduled meeting (six to eight minutes long) to discuss important matters. Don't look for capitulation; if he simply lets the idea begin to enter his head, you've made a big gain. He needs time to think over your viewpoint.

- Be kind and be generous; never descend into pettiness or personal attacks.

- Give abundant praise and approval for things he does well.

- Keep him healthy. He may not think about it.

- Handle the aspects of life together that fall outside the Alpha Male's work-life, so he can give his full attention to that. An Alpha Male *is* his job.

- Winning — every time — is central to an Alpha Male. Help him to do this; never impede him (if you think his goals are wrong, discuss it in a scheduled meeting).

- Make him feel appreciated and cherished. Put him first. Take care of him. Why should an Alpha Male take care of you unless you make his life better, not worse?

- Give him a compliment every day.

- Keep a slight aura of mystique. Never let an Alpha Male think he knows all there is to know about you. Keep him slightly off balance by developing new interests and skills throughout your life together. It will make him wonder what *else* he doesn't know about you.

Is an Alpha Male for you?

If you like excitement and living large, married life with the Alpha Male of your choice is definitely the best of all possible worlds. Life with an Alpha Male will be more varied and interesting (with a greater possibility of your having a job you actually like doing, thanks to the high earning power of most Alpha Males), than life with almost any other man.

The key to success with an Alpha Male is the subject of this book; you don't have to be the most striking-looking or even the most brilliant woman — you can find, train, and marry an Alpha Male, if you go about it in the right way.

If an Alpha Male is for you, we hope you will put the information in this book to good use to find, marry, train, and live happily ever after with the Alpha Male you choose. He will be lucky to have you for his trainer and handler, because you will truly understand him and know how to make him very, very happy. And life with a happy Alpha Male can be more fun than you can imagine!

EPILOGUE

My husband – the author 'XY' of this book — was the quintessential Alpha Male. He fought on Omaha Beach in World War II and some of the other toughest battles of that war and survived against all odds. Through his leadership, many of the soldiers who fought under his command — his 'pack' — are alive today who otherwise wouldn't have made it. Many of the insights of this book come from him.

One day not long ago he noticed shortness of breath, and had trouble standing up. Tests diagnosed lymphoma, a sometimes-curable form of cancer. He went through chemotherapy, but he had toughed it out for too long. The tiredness he had felt — and ignored, being an Alpha Male — had been a symptom of something much worse. It had progressed too far.

Two days before he died of internal bleeding my husband cried out in pain, the first and last time I ever heard him do it. He said in a strangled voice, "*I can't take any more of this.*" A few moments elapsed, and he grinned slightly and said, "You know, you *say* you can't take any more, but you can *always* take a little more."

I had heard of cases in which dying people tell their partner, "Don't be a martyr over this. When I'm gone, I want you to get married again. I don't expect you to remain alone for the rest of your life." My husband didn't say anything like this, and I didn't know what he thought.

But I wanted him to know what *I* thought. Just before he died I told him, "I've never known anyone like you. I've never loved anyone like you. And I'll never get married again."

He looked at me for a long moment. Then he smiled crookedly. "*Good,*" he said.

An Alpha Male to his last breath.

Made in the USA
Lexington, KY
23 June 2011